THE MISSION AND MEDIUM
OF
The Holy Spirit

BY
FOY E. WALLACE, JR.

Charleston, AR:
COBB PUBLISHING

2018

The Mission and Medium of the Holy Spirit was copyrighted © 1968 by Foy E. Wallace, Jr.

Republished with permission.

Published in the United States of America by:

Cobb Publishing
704 E. Main St.
Charleston, AR 72933
(479) 747-8372
CobbPublishing@gmail.com
www.CobbPublishing.com

ISBN: 978-1-947622-14-2

Contents

Prefatory 1
Introductory 5
The Mission and Medium of the Holy Spirit 7
One: The Current Holy Spirit Crusade 9
Two: The Spirit and the Word 21
Three: The Gift of the Holy Spirit 52
Four: The Special Gifts of the Holy Spirit 64
Five: An Exposition of the Holy Spirit Passages 69
Six: The Baptism of the Holy Spirit 114
Seven: The Sin Against The Holy Spirit 129
Conclusion 137

Prefatory

One of the great questions of theology is the mission and medium of the Holy Spirit. This question would be much easier to understand if we had a clearer grasp of the nature of the Godhead. There are three that bear witness in heaven: The Father, the Son, and the Holy Spirit, and these three are one. They do not simply agree as a committee; *they are one*.

As one, they have in common the medium of Revelation. It is God's word. It is the word of Christ. It is the "words which the Holy Spirit speaketh." Through it God reveals his will. Through it Jesus imparts his teaching. And through it the Holy Spirit does his work.

God personally dwells in us as his will finds acceptance in our hearts. Christ personally dwells in us as his teachings are followed by our faith. And the Holy Spirit personally dwells in us as we follow the leading of the Spirit through the word.

Jesus explained his own indwelling in these words: "And the sheep hear his voice: and he calleth his own sheep, he goeth before them, and the sheep follow him: for they know his voice. And a stranger they will not follow..." (John 1:3-5). The shepherd personally indwells the sheep. That's the reason why they will not follow another. Another does not indwell them. But this does not mean that the shepherd dwells inside the sheep personally. The shepherd personally indwells the sheep, but he does not dwell inside the sheep in person. Likewise, God, Christ, and the Holy Spirit indwell Christians, but neither of them dwell inside the Christian *in person*.

Brother Foy E. Wallace Jr. has made this crystal clear in this book. His exhaustive research, and analytical approach to the problem of the Holy Spirit's indwelling leaves very little either to the imagination or to doubt. The reader will be profited greatly by this study, which first ran as a thirteen-week series in the Firm Foundation in the spring of 1967.

—Reuel G. Lemmons,
Editor of the *Firm Foundation*,
Austin, Texas.

Brother Foy E. Wallace Jr. has devoted much time to the study of the Bible and vital issues of the day. In the production of his books—Bulwarks of the Faith, God's Prophetic Word—and a booklet on the Holy Spirit, he has laid us all under heavy obligations. I am glad to commend his books to the careful reading and study of the public.

—B.C. Goodpasture,
Editor of the *Gospel Advocate*,
Nashville, Tennessee.

Although I have read in article form only a part of the material in this book, knowing the position of Brother Wallace on the Holy Spirit, I recommend the book for serious study of the subject.

—W.B. West Jr.,
Dean of the Harding College Graduate School,
Memphis, Tennessee.

IN ACKNOWLEDGEMENT of my indebtedness to my friend and brother, Professor James O. Garrett—a scholar and a linguist who converses in several languages, a teacher of professors, who has more exact knowledge of the New Testament Greek than any man among us of past or present time, from whom scholars have sought counsel—who read and approved the manuscript of this treatise dealing with the Greek argument, and who stands by to verify its correctness, and for any further counsel for which we may feel the need.

—Foy E. Wallace, Jr.

Introductory

Every false teacher must, to save his cause, repudiate the Bible as a guide in religion. The Catholics accept the Bible *plus* the Pope. The Mormons accept the Bible *plus* the Book of Mormon and "continuous revelations of the Holy Spirit" to Guide them. Christian Scientists accept the Bible *plus* the "revelation" given to Mary Baker Eddy. She says, "The final revelation" was given to her "in the year 1866."[1] Mrs. Eddy proves her revelation by "witnessing" and "testimonials."[2]

False teachers among us pretend to accept the Bible, but set additional guidelines by their own "inward leadings or directions by the Holy Spirit." This is clearly evident by the writings and speaking of certain ones among us. They are as far removed from the truth as is the Mormon elder who claims special direction and/or the personal indwelling of the Holy Spirit. The Baptist, Catholic, Methodist, Mormon, Holy Roller, Jehovah's Witness, Episcopalian, Christian Scientist, Christian Church preachers, and many of my brethren all claim to have the "personal indwelling" of the Holy Spirit. They all *prove* their contention by the same method. They resort to "testimonials" and "witnessing." Who am I to reject the "testimony" of a Holiness preacher and yet accept the "witnessing" of a gospel preacher? Which of the two has the Holy Spirit? They both present the *same* evidence—"testimonials." If they both are guided by the Holy Spirit, why do they disagree? The fact that all these religious leaders disagree, including those among us, is proof that the spirit leading them is not *Holy*.

Catholics, Mormons, Christian Scientists, and the Holy Rollers will teach their doctrine and accept the consequences. Some

---

[1] *Science and Health With Key to the Scriptures,* page 107, 1906 edition
[2] *Ibid,* page 600

of my brethren are making the same arguments but *refuse* to accept the consequences. However, their disciples are now bringing their practice into harmony with their doctrine. If this situation is ever corrected, it will have to be corrected at the *source.* Brethren will have to see to it that the truth is taught. If the truth is taught, we need not fear the consequences.

This book is a concise, clear and *correct* exegesis of the passages pertaining to the Holy Spirit and His work. Elders of the church are to guard the flock and protect the brethren against false teachers (Acts 20:28-31). Brethren ought not to support false teaching regardless of *who* teaches it, nor *where* it is taught.

Elders of the church would do well to buy this book by the hundreds and pass them out, not only to the brethren but to prospective members. Every person who is baptized from a denomination needs to read this book because he has been taught false doctrine about the Holy Spirit. That is the reason he was in a denomination in the first place. Our Christian colleges would do well to see to it that every professor and every preacher in school has a copy of this book. If this Baptist doctrine concerning the Holy Spirit is not checked, we are in for a complete apostasy in the church.

—G.K. Wallace,
Vice-President, Freed-Hardeman College.

The Mission and Medium of the Holy Spirit

In the realm of religion there is an affectation known as *Pietism*. It is an esoteric system that originated in Germany as a religious movement in the seventeenth century. The distinctive tenet of this inner circle society was an emphasis on the devotional over the intellectual, based on *emotional experience*. The modern *Pietist* is an adherent of this medieval theology of *Pietism* in the form of an excessive religiosity. It is not piety, nor a synonym for it, nor a derivation of it. The term Pietism is the cognomen for that religious belief—the designation for the principles and practices of the class of persons who advocate an immediate experiential sanctification, a sentimentalism that substitutes feeling for intellect, a substitution of a religion of *feeling* for the religion of the *will*.

The personal attitudes of the modern devotees of Pietism conform to the manner of its founders in the peculiar complex of the parent group—the original Pietist cultus. In early denominational circles, and among some current cults, it appears in the notions of "heartfelt religion," which in the old phraseology is "better felt than told." From the earliest recollections of gospel preaching in the history of the church of the past and present century, gospel preachers have unanimously opposed this so-called "religious experience" and consistently rejected all such psychic emotionalism as evidence of pardon and sanctification or of the indwelling Spirit. It was the preaching of these pioneers of the gospel that drove the "mourner's bench" out of vogue. It is a curious enigma, indeed, that people and preachers within the church now, who should know the truth on the age-old doctrinal controversy over "a religion of the head or of the heart," have now turned Pietists. Their entire argument for direct spiritual influence by an immediate Holy Spirit indwelling is Pietistic—it is governed by sentimental emotions rather than by the consistent evidence of the truth as revealed in the gospel.

It is for the sake of "the truth of the gospel" in the divine plan of salvation, made known to us by the revelation of the Holy Spirit through the written word, that this study of the mission and operation of the Holy Spirit is submitted.

Chapter One:
The Current Holy Spirit Crusade

The extent to which this "Operation Holy Spirit" has developed is evident in the wave of emotionalism across the nation which is crystallizing into a new movement within our ranks. The promoters of it have had a field day, without significant or effective opposition, through the printed mediums extending from California to Tennessee, in articles full of error—some of which could be adapted and printed without comment or exception in a Holiness magazine and in most of the denominational publication organs.

The emphasis of this revolutionary movement is on the *activities* of the Holy Spirit apart from the *Word*. The examples claimed for such extra-curricular activities are such as the "Holy-Spirit-led exodus" to New York and New Jersey, a leader of which claimed "Holy Spirit protection" when he joined the Chicago marchers in the racial demonstration; and another who could not attract a hearing on a New York street corner claimed Holy Spirit direction to another corner several blocks away where a ready audience awaited him; and one who was attending a party was told by the Holy Spirit to leave the table and go to a man who would receive his teaching. Other such incidents ascribed to "activities" of the Holy Spirit recently related are such as the Holy Spirit causing a preacher to miss his plane connection in a city which resulted in teaching a particular person—but that city had several resident gospel preachers and the Spirit could as well have sent one of them—and, then the preacher who was in a rush prayed for the Holy Spirit to reserve a parking place for him in a congested city business block—and it was waiting for him at the right time and place. So we have a new formula—pray and *park*. In these *activities* they really have the Holy Spirit *buzzing* about.

Yet more serious, because of its source and general acceptance, is the claim of preaching by *direct impression* of the Holy Spirit apart from the Word itself, of which there have been numerous instances, the most notable and more representative of this movement being the public declaration of one evangelist that before rising to preach he had prayed for *the Holy Spirit to enter into him.* This action raises many questions: How would the Holy Spirit so suddenly enter him—and what could the Holy Spirit tell him to preach that he could not have learned in the Word of God?

A STRANGE TERMINOLOGY

From the school of this new movement comes a new dialect, a shibboleth, a peculiar vocabulary—that is, new to all members of the church who have ever known the truth as it is taught in the New Testament. Members of the church have lately been exhorted to come forward and "witness for Jesus," and to give "testimonials" of what the Holy Spirit has done for them in "personal experience"—apart from the Word. It is quite common to hear such phraseology as "total commitment" and "total dedication"—and "total Holy Spirit possession"—a theological terminology full of unscriptural connotations never before employed by gospel preachers and discerning church members. This denominational diction stems from the Trueblood book, entitled "The Company of the Committed," being recommended to churches and used in Vacation Bible Schools, though its author is a denominationalist who, not knowing the truth, could not teach the truth.

It is argued that this special activity of the Holy Spirit in the form of direct impression "illuminates" the scriptures and helps the preacher to understand "the written word." That is precisely what Ellen G. White, the prophetess and female pope of the Seventh Day Adventists claimed for herself—the claim of direct illumination. Hear her:

> "The fact that God has revealed his will to men through his word has not rendered needless the continued presence and guidance of the Holy Spirit. On the contrary, the Spirit was promised by our Saviour to open the word to his servants, to illuminate and apply its teachings."[3]

Prophetess Ellen said it with better *illumination* than the young reformers among us. This clique of Holy-Spirit-impressed preachers among us cannot explain the difference of a gnat's eyelash between their form of inspiration and that which was claimed by prophetess Ellen—they had as well join the Adventists. The Holy Spirit wrote the Bible but failed to illuminate it!?

Another point that is being prattled by this school of self-styled Spirit-guided preachers is the demand for "relevancy" in preaching—"we need to make the Bible relevant"—it must be *updated,* we are informed. So said Joseph Smith, the prophet of Mormonism—he taught that the Bible is out of date and that he was Spirit-guided in the task of making revelation relevant. All religious imposters have made that claim, but it is a strange dialect within the church of Christ.

THE PERSONAL EXPERIENCE PRETENSION

In this new outcropping of Holy Spirit emotionalism, its promoters advocate an admittedly mystical experience. In the preaching of *personal experience* these young zealots are not praising the Holy Spirit, they are extolling themselves in the pretended possession of a deeper spiritual devotion than ordinary people experience. In a printed medium of considerable circulation, it has been declared with dramatics that this indwelling of the Holy Spirit apart from the Word is in fact *mystical* but that it does not imply that the Word is incomplete and insufficient—but it does imply *just that;* from it no other inference can be drawn—

---

[3] Preface to *The Great Controversy.*

and the two statements are contradictory and irreconcilable. It is reaching out for *something* they cannot explain; for a *feeling* that is not provable; for a possession which they cannot describe—and the necessary inference and consequence is that the Word of God is incomplete, inadequate, and insufficient. Such teaching is a reversion to that mystical and mystified, mysterious and incomprehensible, unintelligible and intangible religion that is better felt than told. It is the same sort of religion claimed by the Holiness and Nazarenes—and on the same evidence! They deny to the Pentecostals, Holiness, and Nazarenes the same asserted "personal experience" on the same asserted evidence.

This Holy Spirit coterie of preachers and professors among us will deny to these fanatical cults what they claim for themselves on equal experimental evidence, and equally unprovable. These errors have been common to all *orthodox* and *unorthodox* denominations, known by some as an "experience of grace" that the Bible does not define and therefore must be mysteriously received. These late comers will demur when faced with these mysticisms by "the fanatical cults"—but they cannot define the difference. What would they do in debate with them? They had as well join the Holy Rollers.

The conclusion of the whole matter is that no one claiming the personal indwelling or illumination of the Holy Spirit can express a truth, or a true thought or sentiment, on the subject of spiritual influence not already revealed in *the written Word of God.* The concept that an indwelling illumination is necessary would mean that the Holy Spirit wrote a Book—the Bible—but must still directly illuminate us to understand what he wrote! So teach all of these *Holy Ghost* cults; so taught Prophetess Ellen and Imposter Joe—the answer to them will be the answer to themselves.

These errors have been the common ground for all the cults of Adventism and Millennialism. Among us it is the backlash of the millennial influence. The Boll Movement embraced it. In the Neal-Wallace Discussion, Neal claimed direct indwelling of the Spirit and prayed "in the power of the Holy Spirit" before his speech in each session. If true, it would have been rebellion against the Holy Spirit to negate his propositions, but this writer did so and disproved them. Yet he had the same "personal experience" evidence for the *indwelling Holy Spirit.* In the Fort Worth Debate, J. Frank Norris claimed the same "personal experience" and direct indwelling and had his scotchers shouting, and he offered the same mysterious evidence of *personal experience.* Let these men among us answer them, and they answer themselves. This writer did answer them, and the churches of Christ and the preachers of the gospel by the thousands supported him.

But now a Holy Spirit crusader among us has recently declared that he believes in the imminent advent of Christ, for *the early church* believed it—why not he? If it is true that the early church believed the doctrine, they believed an error, for his coming was not imminent—so why shall he not believe the same error? Pshaw! The apostle Paul corrected these errors among some of the early disciples, and both Paul and Peter *knew* that the Lord would not return in their life span, for they both wrote of the things that they foretold would occur in the churches after their decease and departure. To a young preacher of thirty years, *believing* that Christ will appear during his own life-time, it would set the date around the beginning of the next century—but in the case of a man of eighty, it would set the date within ten years. If an event is imminent, it is impending and ready to occur; and if it does not occur it was not imminent. The Bible does not teach the doctrine of immanency—but a preacher who has the immediate indwelling of the Holy Spirit, may receive the impression *through personal experience,* or by praying for *the Holy Spirit to enter into him* and tell him! This excursion serves to illustrate that there is a doctrinal link between the millennial movement and leaders of the Holy Spirit movement within the church.

THE MODE AND THE MEDIUM

The one who claims personal experience as an evidence of the indwelling Spirit abandons the Bible—he cannot prove it by the *Bible, so* he proves it by *himself.* But that is the personal proof that a Holiness preacher offers, and the same facility that establishes one will establish the similar claims of all the cults.

In the nature of things it is impossible for spirit to contact spirit without medium, except through miraculous process, as upon the prophets of God and the apostles of Christ, and to assert it now is to assume *inspiration.* The influence of the Holy Spirit is either by *direct* entrance into the heart or it is *mediated* by the truth—there is no third method thinkable or possible—nor can it be both. The appeal must be made to the Word of God itself, as the source of revealed truth, on this and all other questions.

That the Spirit of God enlightens and converts sinners; comforts and strengthens saints; that love, joy, peace, longsuffering, gentleness, goodness, meekness, fidelity, self-control, are all the fruit of the Spirit, we learn not from inner consciousness, but from the Word of God. The *modus operandi*—the mode, the medium, the how—is the Word of God. "The Spirit of God is ever present with his truth, operating in it, and through it, and by it," said Alexander Campbell in the debate with Rice. This statement is incontrovertible and unassailable and covers the whole issue. Independent of the Word we could never know "whether there be any Holy Spirit." All the knowledge of God, Christ, salvation, and spiritual influence comes only from the Word of God. Apart from the inspiration of the apostles and prophets it is impossible for spirit to communicate with spirit except through *words.* God and Christ never personally occupied anyone; and for the same reason the Holy Spirit does not personally occupy anyone.

The Holy Spirit is a substantive Being, but the influence is metonymical—that is, the use of one word for another in naming the cause for the *effect,* which means the Word is representative of the Spirit, as it is with the indwelling of God and Christ. It cannot be in the case of any of the three—God, Christ, or the Spirit—a literal, substantive, personal indwelling in a direct supernatural movement upon the soul. If the Spirit dwells in a person directly he must provide direct testimony for that immediate indwelling in the demonstration of it. The very theory of a direct indwelling exists to accommodate the mysterious influence, but it has no proof. It amounts to "I know I have it because I feel it." Now, what is the proof? *As goes the proposition so must be the demonstration.* The inspired men—the apostle Paul and evangelist Philip, for instance—knew that the Holy Spirit was directly in them and they demonstrated it with the power of signs and miracles. How does the preacher who now claims the direct indwelling know it? He cannot demonstrate it, and we cannot allow him to prove it by *himself* with the mere assertion of it. The claim does not differ from the Holy Rollers who are equally as honest in their deceptions and offer the same testimonial experience for proof.

The disparaging reference to *the written word* minimizes the Word of God, and it is a decoy to circumvent the Bible as an all-sufficient guide. Divine revelation began with the inspiration of the Holy Spirit in the apostles and prophets and it was finished in *the written word.* When the Word of God was in the inspired man it required the performance of signs to confirm it and the power of miracles to prove it. Now the Word of God is in the Book—the *written word*—and the direct possession of the Holy Spirit is unnecessary and superfluous. Back of this Holy Spirit movement is the late questioning of professors in the colleges of the verbal *inspiration* of the Scriptures—do we or do we not have the inspired Word of God? If so, is it sufficient, or is extended influence required? The answer to these questions has a distinct bearing on the Holy Spirit issue. And there are two decoyers to lure us away from this bulwark—the mutilation of the Word of God by current modern mistranslations of the Bible, and the present 'direct possession of the Holy Spirit' crusade which undermines its sufficiency. But the verbal inspiration of the Scriptures and their all-sufficiency are our ramparts and *we shall not be moved.*

Now comes the charge that we are anti-Holy Spirit. These are old charges, similar to anti-second-coming-of Christ when we deny and reject the premillennial theory. Paul declared (Rom. 10:17) that faith comes by hearing—is that *anti-faith?* He further declared (Gal. 3:2) that the Galatians received the Spirit by the hearing of faith—was that *anti-Spirit?* The assertion that the Holy Spirit is directly received and possessed through *prayer* and *personal experience* amounts to a claim of superiority to the Galatians who received the Spirit through hearing; and to the Ephesians who had the eyes of the understanding enlightened (Eph. 1:17-18) in the knowledge of the word of truth. The Spirit *enters* into us by hearing and seeing the truth, and it *stays* in us the same way.

Next comes the accusation of "cold intellectualism"—a rather anomalous charge coming from the reputed *intellectuals* among us. The apostle Paul identifies the law of the Spirit with the law of the mind. (Rom. 7:23; 8:2) The law of God is designated the law of the mind because it is addressed to the mind—it pertains to the intellect—and is identical with the law of the Spirit. To the Hebrews (8:10) he said God's law was put into the mind and written in the heart and, interchanging the phrases (10:16), God's law was put into the heart and written in the mind. So by this interchange the heart and the mind are made synonymous and, therefore, *heart* religion is *mind* religion. The theory of the immediate impression and possession, and the direct entrance and indwelling of the Holy Spirit, to lead us and guide us, is unintellectual, and therefore contradicts God's law of the mind. God does not circumvent the faculties of his creatures in nature or in grace. So the animated *and* excitatory declaration of a young Paul Revere that *both prayer and providence are at stake* is a false alarm. They are separate subjects in different categories. How God's providence is dispensed through natural law, and how God controls circumstances in answer to prayer, have no bearing on the fallacy of the personal Holy Spirit dwelling in us. We have no scriptural authority or precedent to pray for some of the things mentioned as examples to support direct operation, and a study of the model Disciples Prayer, with proper modification of its preparatory element, may still "teach us how to pray."

A COALITION OF LIBERAL ELEMENTS

It appears that a combination of professors and young evangelists, with the aid of numerous printed mediums, have formed a confederation to stampede the brotherhood and take over the church for the Holy Spirit Movement, similar to and equal to the millennial movement, and as theoretically wrong. It is in fact a doctrinal defection. Like the millennialists, they seek prestige for their cause by fragmentary sentence-quotations from the pioneers. The fluid views of the early restorationists, emerging from denominationalism, may easily be misused, including Alexander Campbell, but by his own words we will deliver him from this modern movement. One writer has backed away from his misapplications of Lipscomb and Boles, and we will have them walking backward on others they have misused, and misapplied.

There are college professors who have been heard to say that the older preachers have not had the scholarship to determine the teaching of the Bible, so the professors assume the prerogative to decide what is the Bible and what is *not* the Bible. In the same vein some young evangelists have expressed the desire to live long enough to undo the damage done to the church by the older preachers on the Holy Spirit question—and one of them averred in my presence before an audience that "the older preachers have not been converted"—and he looked straight at me! Yet these young men stand on the shoulders of the *older preachers,* and but for them they would not now be occupying the pulpits of large congregations where these bombasts have been belched. The whole trouble lies in the fact that the professors are *parroting* the theologians and the young evangelists are *aping* Billy Graham.

Now we are told that the Bible was not translated right. So said Imposter Joseph Smith; so said the digressive scholars of the Christian church on *Psallo* in the instrumental music controversy; so say the liberals now on the word *begotten* in the discussion of the virgin birth of Jesus; so say a growing legion of young modernists who cannot preach the Bible; so say all *who do not like what the Bible says.* Time was when we referred to the Bible everyone knew what was meant—now when the Bible is mentioned everybody is confused for they do not know what is the Bible. It is *the Bible* that made us the people that we are, and the *new bibles* will make us a different people for they are different books. The elders need alerting and the churches need awakening. These spurious bibles are being imposed on them through Literature Series adopting these modern texts, which some churches have returned to the Literature publishers, and which is sufficient ground for all churches to do so.

So the one hundred forty-eight of the world's ripest scholars, the greatest body of translators ever assembled, who produced our old and accepted text, must now give place to the group of neo-orthodox modernists of the late pseudo-versions, and their impositions are being forced and foisted on the churches through professors in and students from the colleges. Among the theologians there exists a mania for revisionism, and its seeds have found soil in our own schools and churches.

Believe it or not, all of this forms a connection by the association of thought with the theorem of mysticism in religious experience, by direct reception and indwelling of the Holy Spirit. The Chairman of the Translating Committee for the Revised Standard

Version is the witness on this point. He is the Doctor Luther Weigle, of Union Theological Seminary, in New York. After stating that the RSV is "the official version" of the National Council of Churches—the *official* NCC Bible—he deposes as follows:

> "A simple statement of the case for the Revised Standard Version is to be found in the Introduction which appeared separately at the time of publication. But the test lies not in abstract argument: It is found in experience."

The *Introduction* to which he refers (1946 edition) objected to "a mechanically exact, literal, word-for-word translation, which follows the order of the Greek words." An exact and accurate wording of the Scriptures is what Chairman Weigle calls "abstract argument," and he substitutes "experience" for exact word-for-word translation—it means that the new version subordinates faithful translation *to personal religious experience.* Herein is the juncture, the concurrence and convergence of the personal experience of direct indwelling with the new version, and therein is the momentum given to the current Holy Spirit crusade.

REGARDING DIRECT DIABOLIC INDWELLING

As an approach to direct indwelling of "the personal Holy Spirit" it has been asserted that in the time of Christ demons entered directly into people, and that the personal devil now has the power of direct entrance into and indwelling within the human heart. The point blank assertion is here made, without proof, that the devil has the power to perform direct operations on the heart of man. It is a bare and naked assertion—we deny it emphatically. The devil operates through the influence of his agents, who are called the ministers of Satan (2 Cor. 11:13-15) operating through *deceitful works;* and through *wicked devices* (2 Cor. 2:11); and by the *agency of a messenger* (2 Cor. 12:7); and by his *devilish wiles* (Eph. 6:11); and by use of the lure, a *diabolical snare* (1 Tim. 3:7; 2 Tim. 2:26); by his subtlety through his *words* mother Eve was *beguiled* (2 Cor. 11:3); and through his agents he deceived the whole world (Rev. 12:19). Thus it is that the devil operates through words and works, devices and doctrines, and through ministers to employ his means and methods of deception—all of which may be *resisted* (1 Pet. 5:8) by one who is "steadfast in the faith." The professor's *devilish* argument boomerangs—for if the personal Satanic possession proves the personal Holy Spirit indwelling, the opposite disproves it. Neither *demon* nor *deity* can personally enter the human heart.

As for demon possession in the time of Christ it is evident that such phenomena belonged to the dispensation of miracles for the purpose of demonstrating the power of Christ over the hadean world. The miraculous incident of casting the devils out of the two that possessed them, and sending them into the herd of swine (Mat. 8:28-33), is an example. There is no evidence of the existence of such possession and casting out of demons before the time of Christ, nor after the apostolic period, and there is no existence of such phenomena today—the conclusion therefore is that demon possession existed for a special purpose and ceased with the miraculous age. Whether true or not, it has no bearing on Holy Spirit indwelling, and the mention of it served only to becloud the issue and to bewilder the readers.

Chapter Two:
The Spirit and the Word

It is here proposed in the form of a proposition that whatever influence is ascribed to the Holy Spirit *within us* in the New Testament is affirmed also of the Word of God. From this vantage ground we proceed to prove that the Holy Spirit operates upon and within the heart of man only *through the Word.*

A certain college professor writes that he had heard of a certain preacher who declared that there are twenty-five such influences and workings of the Holy Spirit which are attributed also to the Word of God. In order to disrobe the anonymity, and to let all men know by the following, who made the declaration[4], we shall herewith list all of these "activities of the Spirit" upon and within us that the Word of God is also said to accomplish, with a *chapter and verse* substantiation.

The professor concedes in advance that "most, if not all" of these things are affirmed of both the Spirit and the Word, but that they are performed separately as when two persons give or do the same thing for another person. On this point the professor gets silly. According to the illustration the Spirit does these things for us separate and apart from the Word, and in turn the Word does these same things for us separate and apart from the Spirit. The illustration has made *two persons* of the Spirit and the Word, and by it the Word is made a person. The illustration has the Spirit per se (by or of itself intrinsically) and the word *per se* (by or of itself intrinsically), acting as two independent persons, thereby denying any agency or instrumentality on the part of either, as in the case of two persons acting separately without the other, doing the same thing for the recipient, another person. It is plain sophistry. But these are the men who talk of fallacy and specialize in

---

[4] i.e., it was Foy E. Wallace, Jr., who was being referenced.—Editor.

such phrases as *illogical argument* and *irresponsible exegesis*. A professor who makes such an illustration is disqualified as either a logician or a scholar.

The Word of God is not a person, it is a medium—and two persons are not giving or doing the same things *to* or *in* us twice at different times. In that illustrative situation one could not know whether it was the Spirit or the Word performing it. The Holy Spirit is the substantive Being, the Person—and it is the *One Spirit* accomplishing these things through the medium of the Word. This is the one thing that has been ignored—the *modus operandi,* the mode and method, the means and medium.

In the Campbell-Rice debate, Alexander Campbell said: "On the subject of spiritual influence there are two extremes of doctrine. There is the *word alone system,* and there is the *Spirit alone system.* I believe in neither." And we believe in neither; but the illustration of the professor has him operating both extremes of the Campbell quotation, for in the case cited, the Spirit is operating apart from the Word and the Word is operating apart from the Spirit, doing the same things at different times. He has stumbled into the inconsistency of adopting both extremes. In the *Christian System,* on page 49, Campbell writes as follows:

> "Christians are, therefore, clearly and unequivocally temples of the Holy Spirit; and they are quickened, animated, encouraged, and sanctified by the power and influence of the Spirit of God, working in them through the truth"

Working in them through the truth. Here the proposition that he affirmed in debate with Rice—in *conviction, conversion, and sanctification, the Holy Spirit operates only through the word*—is applied to Christians. There are numerous whole quotations from his pen by which to prove that Campbell did not teach the indwelling of the Holy Spirit *apart from the word.* Nor did the "majority of the pioneers" so teach, as has been asserted. Alexander Campbell and others have been misrepresented on the Holy Spirit question by incomplete quotations, as we shall show in a later section of this treatise.

No one believes more firmly than this writer that true religion is begun, carried on, and completed by the Holy Spirit—but it is continued and completed in the same way that it begins—through *the Word.* The phrase "through the Word" does not mean the *Word only.* The preposition *through* expresses medium—it is the Spirit working through the Word. There is a wide difference between 'the word only' and the phrase *'only through the word,'* and common honesty behooves certain preachers and professors—and some papers and bulletins—to desist in making false charges and discontinue their misrepresentations.

CONCERNING THE PERSONAL HOLY SPIRIT

There has been much emphasis and constant stress placed on the statement that "the personal Holy Spirit dwells in us"—but the arrangement of the sentence is subtle. The word "personal" is put on the wrong end—the question is: does the Holy Spirit dwell in us *personally?* Compare it with the personal God and the personal Christ—they are persons, but it is admitted that neither God nor Christ dwells in us personally. If that is true in regard to God and Christ, why not in reference to the Holy Spirit? God is in us, Christ is in us, and the Holy Spirit is in us—but they cannot be separated in the representative medium, the *Word of God.*

But we are told that this concept puts the Holy Spirit back in heaven doing nothing. Since it is admitted that Christ does not dwell in us personally, but representatively, the same reasoning would put Christ back in heaven doing nothing—if not, why not? It is a poor rule that will not work both ways. The idea that God remained in heaven, that Christ returned to heaven, but the person of the Holy Spirit is in the world *buzzing about* in all the "activities" that are being imputed to him, separates the Godhead, and is contrary to reason and revelation. The personal God could not enter and dwell in man—it would *burn him up,* for he "only hath immortality, dwelling in the light which no man can approach unto; whom no man hath seen nor can see," said Paul (1 Tim. 6:16); and God said to Moses (Ex. 33:20) "there shall be no man see my face and live." The idea of the personal God, the personal Christ or the personal Holy Spirit dwelling in a man is a theological mis-concept. We receive God *spiritually;* we receive Christ *spiritually;* we receive the Holy Spirit *spiritually.* Here, as Moses, we should stand on holy ground, but this ground is being trampled with hobnail boots!

It will still be insisted that the Bible plainly says that the Holy Spirit dwells in us—verily so, and we believe every passage that says so. But citing the multiple verses is a useless effort, for once the *medium* is established, it applies to them all. It represents the method of argument employed by every denominational preacher and debater:

1. The Bible plainly says that we are saved by faith—but it does not say that we are saved by faith *apart from obedience in baptism.* That is the passage the denominationalist cannot produce.
2. The Bible plainly says that the Holy Spirit dwells within us—but it does not say that the Spirit dwells in us *apart from the Word.* That is the passage that none of these brethren have produced, and they cannot do so.

Paul said (Heb. 4:12) "For the word of God is *quick* (living), and *powerful* (active), and sharper than any two-edged sword, piercing even to the dividing asunder of soul and spirit, and of joints and marrow, and is a discerner of the thoughts and intents of the heart." The disparaging reference to *the written word* is the old theological phraseology borrowed from the seminaries where these men obtained their Divinity degrees, and it is not gospel talk. It can only mean that the Holy Spirit is working outside of the Word—and what these men are saying is that *the word of God is a dead letter.* It is that old denominational refrain that was answered years ago by "the older preachers" all over Tennessee, Arkansas, Oklahoma, and Texas. And that was the "damage to the church on the Holy Spirit question" that some youths in the church have pledged themselves to undo. They need trimming down to size.

It is needless to repeat what no one disputes: That there is an indwelling of the Holy Spirit within the heart of a Christian which operates in his life. But since no one denies it, the crux of the whole discussion is the *modus operandi,* the mode and the medium, or the how of the *indwelling* that abides within and the *outgoing* that flows into the outward living.

The answer is found in the Word of God, for without it we could not know anything about the Holy Spirit at all, nor any of his workings, to which repeated references have been made in the less honoring term of "activities," which to me does not comport with the high office and exalted dignity of the Holy Spirit. It has a degrading effect and connotes a condescension incongruent with Deity.

But we have been told that "not all of the activities of the Holy Spirit are ascribed to the word"—to which we reply that no one has ever so averred. What divine offices and administrations have been assigned to the Holy Spirit in the presence of God among the angels in heaven is not the point, and it has no place in these discussions.

There are only two ways that the Holy Spirit could influence men; first, the immediate—it means no intermediary, no medium, a bearing down on the object without any intervening medium; second, the mediate—through an intervening instrument or agent by which a thing is accomplished, not direct. The immediate influence was upon the prophets of God and the apostles of Christ for the purpose of inspiration. The direct indwelling calls for the direct expression—for why a direct indwelling without the direct expression and guidance? The *tongues movement* is the immediate outgrowth of that very thing, and the theory of direct indwelling is responsible for it. But the *mediate* influence of the Holy Spirit upon the minds of others than the inspired man is through the intervening instrument of the inspired word.

A RULE OF EXEGESIS

There is a method of deciding things that is commonly called a rule, and when established it is a basis upon which to determine things within its classification. As applied to the present case when the rule that governs the operation medium of the Holy Spirit is once established, the purport of all passages bearing on it must be construed in harmony with the established rule. There are two clear examples of this rule:

First: When it is established that baptism is for the remission of sins, as stated in Acts 2:38, that design is implied when or where baptism is mentioned elsewhere, and must be so understood. It is not necessary to repeat the design with every occurrence or mention of baptism.

Second: When it is established that the design of the Lord's Supper is in order to the memory of Christ, that design is implied wherever the institution is mentioned, and must be so understood. It is not necessary to repeat the design with every reference to the Lord's Supper.

On the same principle, when it is established that the *modus operandi* of the Holy Spirit upon or within us, is through the Word of God—comparably, that medium is implied wherever the Spirit's influence upon or within us is mentioned, and must be so understood. It is not necessary to repeat the medium with every reference to the Spirit's operation and indwelling—all other passages must be construed in harmony with the established medium. This being undeniably true in the examples of baptism and the Lord's Supper, it is plainly true respecting the operation medium of the Holy Spirit. "By the same rule let us walk."

There are multiple scriptures on the operation, indwelling and leading of the Holy Spirit that can be aggregated—we believe them all, and if there are any more to be found, we believe them too, but the solution will be the same. Howbeit, it is our purpose to examine, one by one, in this syllabus of the subject, every passage of scripture that has been appropriated to the direct personal indwelling and to prove that they have all been misappropriated.

THE TWENTY-FIVE POINTS

But now—those twenty-five particulars, and the propositional premise: The fact that every effect and influence that the Holy Spirit exerts upon and within us is affirmed of the Word of God proves that the Spirit operates only through the Word—that every effect or emotion that the Holy Spirit generates within us, the Word of God engenders.

1. The spiritual *begetting* is with the Word.

> *"Of his own will begat he us with the word of truth, that we should be a kind of first-fruits of his creatures"—Jas. 1:18.*

> *"For though ye have ten thousand instructors in Christ, yet have ye not many fathers: for in Christ Jesus I have begotten you through the gospel"—1 Cor. 4:15.*

All life is generated through *seed.* When the Word—the spiritual seed—is planted in the heart, it germinates on the same principle as the corn that is deposited in the earth. The Word has in it the embryo of spiritual life. This was according to God's will, the apostle James said, and having thus willed it, God accomplished it with *the word of truth*—and as the apostle Paul put it: *through the gospel.*

2. The spiritual *birth* springs from the incorruptible and eternal Word.

> "Being born again, not of corruptible seed, but of incorruptible, by the word of God, which liveth and abideth forever"—1 Pet. 1:23.

The one born of the Word has a higher birth than natural birth of corruptible seed. The divine Giver implants within the heart the word that is living and everlasting—"which liveth and abideth forever." It is the Word of the living God, and it is His living Word. The fructification of this incorruptible seed is on the principle of the vegetational comparison itself—the germination and development is from the seed. So it is with the spiritual life—the generation and fruition is within and from the seed, the Word of God.

3. The *quickening* of the heart is with the operation of the Word.

> "And you hath he quickened, who were dead in trespasses and sins... even when we were dead in sins, hath quickened us together with Christ, by grace are ye saved"—Eph. 2:1, 5.

Here the process of quickening is that of salvation by grace. But Paul said to Titus (Tit. 2:11-12) that the grace of God that brings salvation *teaches us.* The good words grace and gospel are used synonymously in the New Testament. David declared: Thy word hath quickened me... I will never forget thy precepts: for with them thou hast quickened me"—Psa. 119:50, 93. David's ardent declaration is consonant with Paul's argument of Col. 2:12-13: "Buried with him in baptism, wherein also ye are risen with him through the faith of the operation of God, who hath raised him from the dead. And you, being dead in your sins... hath he quickened together with him, having forgiven you all trespasses." The quickening is the salvation by grace in Eph. 2:1, 5; and of the forgiveness of all trespasses in Col. 2:12-13; and is accomplished by the word of God and its precepts, according to Psa. 119:50, 93. The Spirit quickens when the seed of the Word gets into the moral nature of man as the rudiment from which life springs.

4. The spiritual *cleansing* is a process of the Word.

> *"Now ye are clean through the word that I have spoken unto you"—John 15:2.*

> *"Even as Christ also loved the church, and gave himself up for it; that he might sanctify and cleanse it with the washing of water by the word"—Eph. 5:26.*

This cleansing process is begun *through the word* in the teaching of Christ, and is completed *by the word*—its agency is the inspired teaching of the apostles of Christ.

5. The soul is *purified* in obedience to the Word.

> *"Seeing ye have purified your souls in obeying the truth through the Spirit unto unfeigned love of the brethren, see that ye love one another with a pure heart fervently"—1 Peter 1:22.*

The process of purification is begun by embracing the gospel, and "in obeying the truth." Through the teaching of the Spirit, the indwelling truth springs into all of the virtues of brotherhood in the church. Thus the truth is the effective instrument for the continued purifying of the soul.

> *"And every man that hath this hope in him purifieth himself, even as he is pure"—1 John 3:3.*

6. The soul is *saved* by the implanted Word.

> *"Receive with meekness the engrafted word, which is able to save your souls. But be ye doers of the word, and not hearers only"*—Jas. 1:21-22.

To graft is to insert a limb from one tree into another. In this description the limb of the word is *received,* and is therefore acquired by hearing and doing the teaching. Paul said to the Corinthians: "Moreover, brethren, I declare unto you the gospel which I preached unto you, which also ye have received, and wherein ye stand; by which also ye are saved"—1 Cor. 15:1-2. They had received the same engrafting of the gospel and were in the state of salvation—"By which ye are saved." But James exhorts the saved members to receive with meekness the word which is able to save—that by the hearing and the doing of the doctrine of the gospel, the implanted word, they would remain in the state of salvation—the word is able *to keep us saved,* if we continue to hear it and do it.

7. The *justification* by faith comes through obedience to the Word.

> *"For not the hearers of the law are just before God, but the doers of the law shall be justified"*—Rom. 2:13.

> *"Knowing that a man is not justified by the works of the law, but by the faith of Jesus Christ, even we have believed in Jesus Christ, that we might be justified by the faith of Jesus Christ."*—Gal. 2:16.

On the basis of a general principle or truth, justification comes not to hearers only but to doers; the law was here used as an illustration, but the justification comes through "the law of faith," not by the boasted works of the law of the Jews. "Where is boasting then? It is excluded. By what law? of works? Nay: but by the law of faith"—Rom. 3:27. What is here described as *the law of faith* by which all are justified is designated in the Galatian letter as *the faith of* Christ—"Even we have believed in Jesus Christ, that we might be justified by the faith of Christ." The clauses "the faith of Christ" and "the law of faith" mean the gospel—and being "justified by the Spirit of our God," in 1 Cor. 6:11, is justification by the gospel.

8. It was the apostle's desire for all to be *filled* with knowledge.

> *"That ye might be filled with the knowledge of his will in all wisdom and spiritual understanding"—Col. 1:9.*

It was "through the power of the Holy Spirit—verse 18—that the knowledge of his will had come to them for the source of spiritual understanding. It can come to us and dwell in us only through the teaching of the truth—verse 5—"wherefore ye heard before in the word of the truth of the gospel"—and that means *only through the Word.*

9. The members of the church were given inspired instruction to let the *Word* dwell in them.

> *"Let the word of Christ dwell in you richly in all wisdom; teaching and admonishing one another in psalms and hymns and spiritual songs, singing with grace in your hearts to the Lord."—Col. 3:16.*

The parallel passage is Eph. 5:18-19: "Be filled with the Spirit, speaking to yourselves in psalms and hymns and spiritual songs, singing and making melody in your heart to the Lord." The "word of Christ" is the word that he inspired his apostles to preach, and which the members of the body were told to let inhabit their hearts. On the same subject to the Ephesians the apostle commanded that they "be filled with the Spirit." A reading of the two passages side by side will prove the parallel: Be filled with the Spirit—Let the word of Christ dwell in you richly. The sentence structure is the imperative mood—"Be filled with the Spirit" is a command—the imperative mood carries the command. One cannot obey a promise, or that which is bestowed as a gift, such as a direct reception or an immediate indwelling of the Holy Spirit; therefore the instruction to *be filled with the Spirit* does not refer to a direct indwelling of the Holy Spirit. The passage in Ephesians is a command and the parallel Colossian passage, *let the word of Christ dwell in you richly,* describes *how* the command is obeyed. Thus Eph. 5:18 and Col. 3:16 are equated, and to be 'filled with the Spirit' is accomplished through the Word.

10. The means of direction and guidance is that of being *led* by the Word.

> *"Thou shalt guide me with thy counsel, and afterward receive me to glory"*—Psa. 73:24.
>
> *"Thy word is a lamp unto my feet, and a light unto my pathway"*—Psa. 119:105.
>
> *"To give knowledge of salvation unto his people... to give light to them that sit in darkness... to guide our feet in the way of peace"*—Luke 1:77-79.

These passages encircle and encompass the word of God. All who are guided by the Word are led by the Spirit, and his word is able to lead us to heaven: "Thou shalt guide me with thy counsel, and afterward receive me to glory."

11. The *witness* within the heart of true believers is the Word of Truth.

> *"And it is the Spirit that beareth witness, because the Spirit is truth"—1 John 5:6.*

It is claimed that the statement of verse 10, "He that believeth on the Son of God hath witness in himself," establishes the immediate indwelling of the Holy Spirit. But the context declares what this witness is and how it is received: "If we receive the witness of men, the witness of God is greater: for this is the witness of God which he hath testified of his Son." The witness of men is their uninspired testimony of human consciousness. But the witness of God, which is greater than man, is the inspired testimony of the truth. The proper reading of verse 10 verifies it: "He that believeth on the Son of God hath witness in himself: he that believeth not God hath made him a liar; because he believeth not the record that God gave of his Son"—*believeth not the record*—and the record is the Word. The terms *witness, testify,* and *record,* clearly show that the truth is the sphere in which the witness exists—it is the gospel of witness. There is nothing in the passage that affirms an immediate indwelling of the Spirit or that describes the naked Spirit of God operating on the naked spirit of man without testimony—and the testimony is the truth, and the witness is the inspired Word of Truth.

12. The *growth* of the spiritual babe is by the milk of the Word.

> *"As newborn babes desire the sincere milk of the Word, that ye may grow thereby"—1 Pet. 2:1.*

The reference to the newborn babes connects with the immediate context of the preceding verse 1:23—"Being born again, not of corruptible seed, but of incorruptible; by the word of God. As newborn babes, desire the sincere milk of the word, that ye may grow thereby." The *sincere milk* means the pure unadulterated Word; and *grow thereby* means that the Word is all-sufficient to accomplish the end of spiritual growth. All to whom the apostle was writing had been saved from past sins, and the pure and unadulterated Word was all that was necessary to accomplish their present, future and final salvation.

13. The effectual *working* within is accomplished by the indwelling Word.

> *"For this cause also thank we God without ceasing, because, when ye received the word of God which ye heard of us, ye received it not as the word of men, but, as it is in truth, the word of God, which effectually worketh also in you that believe"*—1 Thess. 2:13.

The people to whom Paul was writing had received the word of God by hearing the preaching of it, and this same word was *effectually working* in them. The word *effectual* means, according to its definition: that which is powerful enough to produce the intended effect, adequate—it is fully efficacious—no supplement is necessary. It means that the Word is all-sufficient.

14. The truth within produces *fruit* without.

> *"For the hope which is laid up for you in heaven, whereof ye heard before in the word of the truth of the gospel; which is come unto you... and bringeth forth fruit, as it doth also in you since the day ye heard of it, and knew the grace of God in truth"*—Col. 1:5-6.

What a passage—what a declaration! In one verse are all three terms—the *word*, the *truth*, the *gospel*—in significant order. The Word was heard and believed when it was first preached; it was present *with* them and *in* them in the form of the revealed truth; and it was the gospel, the good news of salvation and of "the hope which is laid up for you in heaven." This living, animated thing, called the *word* and the *truth* and the *gospel* remained in them to produce and bring forth *fruit* continually, making them increasingly fruitful in the knowledge of God. (verses 9 and 10) The three terms—the word, the truth, and the gospel, were as one fertile tree, yielding abundant fruit with increasing knowledge, of which the Colossians were a specimen. This is the "fruit of the Spirit," through the Word.

15. The indwelling truth is the rule by which the followers of Christ *walk* in the doing of his entire will.

> *"I rejoice greatly that I found of thy children walking in truth, as we have received commandment from the Father... This is the commandment, that, as ye have heard from the beginning, ye should walk in it"*—2 John 4.
>
> *"I have no greater joy than to hear that my children walk in truth"*—3 John 4.
>
> *"Nevertheless, whereto ye have already attained, let us walk by the same rule, let us mind the same things"*—Phil. 3: 16.

The word *truth* is mentioned five times in Second John, The truth was *in Gaius* and he loved it and walked in it. There could be no better way of walking in the Spirit than to *walk in the truth*. It is the revelation of the Holy Spirit, and with this word of the Spirit to lead us, we may all with one mind walk by the same rule.

16: The source of *strength* is the knowledge of the Word of His grace.

> *"And now, brethren, I commend you to God, and to the word of his grace, which is able to build you up, and to give you an inheritance among all them which are sanctified"—Acts 20:32.*

> *"That ye may be filled with the knowledge of his will... increasing in the knowledge of God; strengthened with all might, according to his glorious power"—Col. 1:10-11.*

> *"And I myself also am persuaded of you, my brethren, that ye also are full of goodness, filled with all knowledge, and able to admonish one another."—Rom. 15:14.*

The expression "word of his grace which is able to build you up," in Acts 20:32, is equal with "the grace of God that bringeth salvation," in Tit. 2:11-12, which "teaches us"—the grace of God builds us up by teaching us. And we are "strengthened with all might" when we are "filled with the knowledge of his will," according to explanations in Rom. 16:25. And this is how one is "strengthened with might by his Spirit in the inner man" (Eph. 3:16)—it is through "the glorious power" of his Word when we are filled with the knowledge of it.

17. The inspired Word has in it the power to *comfort* the bereaved.

> *"Wherefore comfort one another with these words"—1 Thess. 4:18.*

> *"And sent Timothy, our brother, and minister of the gospel of Christ, to establish you, and to comfort you concerning your faith"—1 Thess. 3:2.*

> *"For whatsoever things were written aforetime were written for our learning, that we through patience and comfort of the scriptures might have hope"—Rom. 15:4.*

In the period of persecution that followed, in the years after these epistles were delivered to these churches, many of their members were martyrs. It is not fanciful to say that their comfort was found in the indwelling words of inspiration. The Scriptures, both Old and New, were written for our learning through which we receive the comfort of hope—and that is *through the Word.*

18. The spirit of *grace* in the apostolic epistles is set forth as the gospel of Christ.

> *"The ministry which I have received of the Lord Jesus, to testify the gospel of the grace of God... and to the word of his grace, which is able to build you up"—Acts 20:24, 34.*

> *"The grace of God which bringeth salvation, teaching us"—Tit. 2:11-12.*

> *"Who hath trodden under foot the Son of God, and hath counted the blood of the covenant, wherewith he was sanctified, an unholy thing, and hath done despite unto the Spirit of grace"—Heb. 10:29.*

It is clear that *grace* in these passages is equated with the *gospel*; and that the spirit of grace in Heb. 10:29 is the New Covenant; and the grace of God that brings salvation is the gospel. Added to these is the marvel that Paul expressed that the Galatians (Gal. 1:6) had so soon removed from the grace of God to another gospel, thus declaring the grace of God to be the gospel; and the qualifying statement, *'which is not another,'* shows that they had removed from the gospel to something that was not the gospel at all. It follows therefore, that the *Spirit of grace* is in us when the word of grace is in us.

19. The love of God is *shed* abroad in our hearts by the gospel.

> *"Lest the light of the glorious gospel of Christ should shine unto the;, for God who commanded light to shine out of darkness, hath shined in our hearts, to give the light of the knowledge of the glory of God in the face of Jesus Christ"*—2 Cor. 4:4-6.

The statement of Rom. 5:5, that the love of God is *shed* in our hearts by the Holy Spirit, and the statement of 2 Cor. 4:4-6 that the light of the knowledge of God is *shined* in our hearts by the gospel, have the same connotation. The prepositional phrase *by the Holy Spirit* simply denotes agency, and that agency is *the glorious gospel.* The words are different but the thought is the same—and *how* the knowledge of God is *shined* in our hearts through the gospel is exactly *how* the love of God is *shed* in our hearts by the Holy Spirit. It is through the Word.

20. The Word is said to *live* within the one who believes it.

> *"I am the bread of life: he that cometh to me shall never hunger.... I am the living bread which came down out of heaven: if any man eat this bread, he shall live forever"*—John 6:35, 51.

In the context between these two verses is the statement: "And they shall all be taught of God. Every man therefore that hath heard, and hath learned of the Father, cometh unto me"—verse 45. It is clear that the bread of life is *eaten,* or received, through being *taught,* and by having *heard,* and by *learning,* and thus through the bread of the *word,* its life is in us. When Paul said that "Christ liveth in me," he further stated that it was "The faith of the Son of God" in him (Gal. 2:20); and no one claims the personal indwelling of Christ in the heart, all admitting that it is representative.

But the *Twentieth Century Christian,* which boasts of a non-controversial policy, has projected its publication into the Holy Spirit controversy by a *Special Number* entitled: *The Holy Spirit Lives In Us,* in which the theological theory of the direct Holy Spirit indwelling was propagandized. But the apostolic statement that *Christ lives in us* is stated word-for-word, yet not one of them claims that it is a direct indwelling of Christ in us—they all concede it to be representative. So this heretofore *non-controversial* publication could as well have produced a *Special Number* entitled: *Christ Lives In Us.* We do not deny either—but we do contend that *The Holy Spirit Lives In Us* in the same way and to the same extent that Christ lives in us, both being representative—and it is inexcusably inconsistent to teach that one is mediate and the other immediate. Christ lives in us in the same way that he enters into us (Gal. 3:2)—through "the hearing of faith." And it is all through the *inspired Word.*

21. The Words spoken by Christ engender *spirituality* in us.

> *"It is the Spirit that quickeneth; the flesh profiteth nothing: the words that I speak unto you, they are spirit and they are life"*—John 6:63.

It is easy to see that the word *spirit* in this text means *spiritual,* and the word *life* means *life-giving*—the words of Christ are *spiritual* and *life-giving*—capable of conveying spirituality. The Holy Spirit cannot make any one "more spiritual" than the spiritual words of Christ can make him.

But another recent publication has the title: *The Holy Spirit and Spirituality,* for to teach that direct Holy Spirit indwelling is necessary to spirituality. It is tantamount to saying that the teaching of the *spiritual words* of Christ cannot make one spiritual!

Both of these recent publications are full of error, and we dare to suggest that the *Twentieth Century Christian* should return to the *first* century for its doctrine, and the other one to the *words of Christ* for spirituality.

22. The Word within the heart *flows* outward into the life.

> *"But whosoever drinketh of the water that I shall give him shall never thirst; but the water that I shall give him shall be in him a well of water springing up into everlasting life."—John 4:14.*

> *"Our fathers did eat manna in the desert; as it is written, He gave them bread from heaven to eat... I am the bread of life: he that cometh to me shall never hunger; and he that believeth on me shall never thirst"—John 6:31-35.*

The water from Jacob's well, and the manna in the desert, had satisfied a want; but *this* well and *this* bread would fill up the measure of *spiritual* want. "If any man eat of this bread, he shall live forever." The springing water and the descending manna were types of the spiritual nourishment in Christ. "And did all eat the same spiritual meat; and did all drink the same spiritual drink; for they drank of that spiritual Rock that followed them: and that Rock was Christ"—1 Cor. 10:3-4. This living bread and living water is the *word of Christ,* for so the Lord himself applied it in the same context: "the words that I speak unto you, they are spirit, and they are life." It is all connected with *eating* the divine food. The prophet said: "Thy words were found and I did eat them"—Jer. 15:16. The psalmist said: "How sweet are thy words to my taste! Yea, sweeter than honey to my mouth!"—Psa. 119:103.

The misused passage of John 7:38-39 has this same import and is in connection with the well of water and the bread of life.

"He that believeth on me, as the Scripture hath said, out of his belly shall flow rivers of living water. (But this spake he of the Spirit, which they that believe on him should receive: for the Holy Spirit was not yet given; because that Jesus was not yet glorified.)" Here the Spirit is explained to mean the rivers of living water flowing, parallel with the well of living water *springing.* It marks an operation of the Spirit and not the personal Holy Spirit. It is metonymical—meaning the use of another word for the same thing, as in Luke 11:13 and Matt. 7:11, where the *Holy Spirit* is put for the *things* the Spirit gives. These passages describe the blessings of salvation which would flow as a perennial stream from the believers *through the divine word.*

In a later analysis of these texts it will be shown that they are a cluster of gospel previews and Pentecost pointers, and are dispensational in their application.

23. The ingress of the Word *enlightens* the heart.

> *"The entrance of thy words giveth light; it giveth understanding to the simple"—Psa. 119:130.*
>
> *"The statutes of the Lord are right, rejoicing the heart; the commandment of the Lord is pure, enlightening the eyes"—Psa. 19:8.*

The terms *entrance* and *statutes* and *commands,* joined with *light* and *eyes* and *understanding* and *rejoicing,* are all faculties of the heart, the mind, and the intellect. They do not denote direct Holy Spirit entrance and action—but the influence of the *living word* upon the heart and within the soul of man.

24. The source of *understanding* is the inspiration of the Word.

> *"But there is a spirit in man: and the inspiration of the Almighty giveth them understanding"—Job*

32:8.

"Through thy precepts I get understanding: therefore I hate every false way"—Psa. 119:104.

"All scripture is given by inspiration, and is profitable for doctrine, for reproof, for correction, for instruction in righteousness: that the man of God may be perfect, throughly furnished unto all good works"—2 Tim. 3:16-17.

Amplifying the foregoing emphasis on the Word as the full source of understanding, it is written in Eph. 1:17-18 that the spirit of wisdom and revelation is given to us through knowledge, and in 3:4 the apostle added: "when ye read ye may understand my knowledge." The recent notion that it requires the direct indwelling of the *personal* Holy Spirit to illuminate the scriptures, so that we may understand them is sheer error. In that case we would have no need of the scriptures at all, as we would all be equal to Paul himself and all of the apostles. The inspired Scripture is complete for doctrine—the teaching of the revealed truth; for reproof—the conviction of error in teaching or in life; for correction—the restoration of the erring to the right way; for instruction in righteousness—the constant teaching of the new believer of all the parts of the divine system of justification, which is the state of righteousness. The divine scriptures throughly furnish us—throughly, through and through—to teach the ignorant, to convict the sinner, to correct the erring, to edify the believer—the inspired *word* is all-sufficient.

25. The work of *sanctification* is completed by the Word.

"Sanctify them through thy truth: thy word is truth"—John 1:17.

The sanctification here implied is the consecration—that setting apart which is accomplished and completed and realized *through the truth.* The word of God is not only true, it is the truth—the sum of revelation. The sanctifying of the apostles in this reference was *through the truth* that was put in them by the revelation of it. To us the sanctification begins with baptism, "with the washing of water," the agency of which is "by the word"—Eph. 5:26: "That he might sanctify and cleanse it with the washing of water by the word." Thus sanctification is the effect of the Word on the heart.

26. Not lending ear to the word is *resisting* the Spirit.

> *"Ye stiffnecked and uncircumcised in heart and ears, ye do always resist the Holy Spirit; as your fathers did, so do ye"—Acts 7:51.*

> *"Yet many years didst thou forbear them, and testified against them by thy spirit in thy prophets: yet would they not give ear"—Neh. 9:30.*

The term *stiffnecked* is an unusual word, occurring one time only in the New Testament, and only seven times in the Old Testament. It has in it all that the word *obstinate* can connote. The term *uncircumcised* conveys the meaning of a covering over the ears which rendered the heart inaccessible to the truth. These terms described the attitude of their fathers toward the word of the prophets—as your fathers did, so do you. The term '*as*' is an adjective, the use of which is to introduce examples and illustrative phrases—and 'as your fathers did,' means that Jews in the audience of Stephen resisted the word of God to the same extent and in the same degree that their fathers had done in resisting the prophets. The term 'so' is an adverb of manner, and it means that the Jews resisted the word that Stephen preached in the same manner in which their fathers had resisted the word of the prophets. The Nehemiah passage states this manner exactly: Their fathers had resisted *the spirit of God* when they rejected *the word* that the prophets had *testified;* and the Jews resisted the *Holy Spirit* when they rejected *the word* that Stephen *preached.* "Now as Jambres and Jannes withstood Moses, so do these resist the truth"—2 Tim. 3:8.

27. The unbelief of the Word is *grieving* the Spirit.

> *"Today if ye will hear his voice, harden not your heart... as in the provocation... forty years long was I grieved with this generation, and said, It is a people that do err in their heart, and they have not known my ways"—Psa. 95: 7-10.*

> *"Wherefore the Holy Spirit saith, Today if you will hear his voice, harden not your hearts, as in the provocation... wherefore I was grieved with that generation... Take heed, brethren, lest there be in any one of you an evil heart of unbelief, in departing from the living God"—Heb. 3:7-12.*

The apostle of Hebrews connects grieving the Spirit of God with the "evil heart of unbelief"—a stubborn attitude toward his word. The evil *heart* expression is characteristic of Jeremiah's indictments of stubbornness against Israel (Jer. 3:17; 7:24; 11:8; 16:12; 18:12). In all of these passages the phrase is preceded by the word *imagination,* which is derived from an original root that signifies *stubbornness.* The callous attitude toward *the word* of God is grieving *the Spirit* of God.

28. The disobedience to the Word is *quenching* the Spirit.

> *"Quench not the Spirit—1 Thess. 5:19.*

> *"And the foolish said unto the wise, Give us of your oil; for our lamps are gone out"—Matt. 25:8.*

It is interesting, indeed, that the words *gone out* are translated from the original word *shennami,* which is exactly the same word from which *quench* is translated in 1 Thess. 5:19: *Quench* not the Spirit. The word conveys the idea of a flame, when it is put out or allowed to go out, it is quenched. Jeremiah said that the word of God is fire: "Is not my word like as fire? saith the Lord"—Jer. 23:29. David said: "My heart was hot within me; while I was musing the fire burned: then spake I with my tongue"—Psa. 93:3. When *the flame of the word* is extinguished the Spirit of God is quenched.

The exhortation of the apostle Paul in 1 Thess. 5:19 to "quench not the Spirit" referred to his own inspired teaching. In their failure to accept and practice Paul's teaching in his epistle to them, the Thessalonians would have thereby quenched the Spirit which was in the inspired teaching of the apostle—and the same is true today, the Spirit is quenched when the inspired Word within us is restrained.

29. The repudiation of the Word is *blaspheming* the Spirit.

> *"But when the Jews saw the multitudes, they were filled with envy, and spake against those things which were spoken by Paul, contradicting and blaspheming"—Acts 13:45.*

Here is the word *blaspheemeo,* the same word employed by Jesus in Mark 3:28:29: "All sins shall be forgiven unto the sons of men, and blasphemies wherewith soever they shall blaspheme: but he that shall blaspheme against the Holy Spirit hath never forgiveness, but is in danger of eternal damnation." It is the same word in the text of 1 Tim. 6:1: "That the name of God and his doctrine be not blasphemed"; and in Tit. 2:5: "That the word of God be not blasphemed." To deny with insult the *doctrine* and treat with scorn *the word* is doing *despite* to the Spirit of grace and is blaspheming the Spirit of God.

30. The body that is interred in the tomb will be *raised* at the last day by the Word of Christ.

> *"For the hour is coming, in the which all that are in the graves shall hear his voice, and shall come forth; they that have done good, unto the resurrection of life; and they that have done evil, unto the resurrection of damnation"—John 5:28-29.*

The Lord himself shall descend from heaven with a shout (1 Thess. 4:16) and by his word the dead shall rise. The voice-shout of the descending Lord is the last trump (1 Cor. 15:52) by which the dead shall be called from hadean habitations. "The Lord himself shall descend with a shout, with the voice of the archangel, and with the trump of God." Our dictionary defines *trump* as an archaic form of triumph—it is *the word of God in triumph* that shall raise the dead.

31. The criterion of the *judgment* will be the Word of Christ.

> *"And if any man hear my words, and believe not, I judge him not: for I came not to judge the world, but to save the world. He that rejecteth me, and receiveth not my words, hath one that judgeth him: the word that I have spoken, the same shall judge him in the last day"—John 12:47-48.*

Here the Lord combines his words in the word—in its entirety, complete and delivered in final form. The clause, "hath one that judgeth him," does not refer to Jesus as verse 47 states, but is a reference to *the word,* of verse 48, which shall judge him—the one who rejects it—in the last day. The Word may be both refused and rejected, but it cannot be expelled; it may be dismissed but it cannot be banished—it will cling to the hearer to judge him.

If the Holy Spirit operates upon or dwells within the heart without the Word, what does he do that is not affirmed of the Word? By direct operation and indwelling of the Spirit apart from the Word, or the Word apart from the Spirit, the agency of one or the other is cancelled—but with the Spirit operating through the Word, both remain. Therefore, said Paul—calling all ministers: *Preach the Word,* and may we all cleave to it.

Now, there are the twenty-five itemizations, with six more for good measure, in the positive proof that *every effect and emotion that the Holy Spirit produces, the Word of God engenders.*

They may continue to chant that the Holy Spirit does it, too—but the incontrovertible conclusion is that the Spirit accomplishes all of it *through the Word.* They may ridicule and belittle it, shrug it off and laugh at it, but they cannot do anything with it. An *oracle* may be issued from Abilene that it is "illogical argument" and "irresponsible exegesis"—*but they cannot answer it.*

ABSTRACTING ALEXANDER CAMPBELL

Due to the reckless and unreliable references that have been made to Campbell on the *direct indwelling* argument, we will make this treatise relevant by subjoining to the thirty-point epitome, on the *Spirit And The Word,* an index to Campbell's printed statements that will set the record straight, and eliminate him as a star witness for the direct operations of the Holy Spirit, upon or within either sinners or saints. Some of the early writers, so close to emergence from denominational theology, were not clear in their conceptions or settled in their views on certain facets of spiritual influences and operations, but not so with Campbell—his declarations all come through loud and clear, in the *Campbell-Rice Debate* and in the *Christian System.*

First: From his affirmative in the debate with the then popular denominationalist Nathan L. Rice, he joined *conviction, conversion,* and *sanctification* together inseparably as the work of the

Holy Spirit, operating only *through the Word.* The following statements are the high points of his argument:

1. The basic argument was drawn from the constitution of the human mind—that the intellectual and moral faculties are the same after as before one becomes a Christian, and that the medium of spiritual influences and operations are also the same.
2. That it is unscriptural, as well as irrational and unphilosophic to discriminate between spiritual agency and instrumentality—between what the Word does and what the Spirit does as though they were distinct powers and influences.
3. That in the proposition—*The Spirit operates only through the Word*—the word 'only' is redundant in denial of the assumption that in regeneration the Spirit operates *sometimes* without the Word, and therefore *only,* by the force of circumstances, is made to mean *always*.
4. That if either conversion or sanctification is effected by the Word of Truth at all, it is by the Holy Spirit through the Word alone.
5. That it is neither the *Spirit alone* nor the *Word alone* operating upon or within the heart—but the Spirit operating *through* the Word.
6. That in the illumination and sanctifying operations of the Spirit there is not a single conception or idea on the whole subject of spiritual things not already found in Holy Scripture, the written word—read of all men who choose to learn what the Spirit of God has said to saints and sinners.
7. That God gave man reason and religion by giving him speech—and taught him the primitive words from which man manufactured the derivatives—so the *Spirit*

of God, which is now the *Spirit of the Word,* is the origin of all spiritual words and conceptions, expressing spiritual things in spiritual words—therefore, in conversion and sanctification the Spirit of God operates only by and through the Word; and based upon the constitution and faculties of the human mind, the influences and operations of the Spirit are the same after as before one becomes a Christian—that *God does not circumvent the faculties of his creatures.*

8. That the work of conversion and sanctification is *begun* and *carried* on and *completed* by the personal agency of the Holy Spirit, and the indwelling presence of the Spirit, through knowledge, belief and obedience, being continued and completed the same way in which it was begun—through the knowledge of the truth and in obedience to it—thus disavowing any direct operation of the Holy Spirit upon or within the soul.

9. As the body, or outward man, has its peculiar organization, so has the mind, or inner man. As the outward man is endowed with physical senses, adapted to a world of sensible, material objects—the inner man is endowed with the faculties of the mind which are adapted to the spiritual system. As the outward man subsists upon material sustenance, so the inner man subsists on the spiritual system, receiving and assimilating whatever is compatible with its faculties—that God feeds and sustains man physically in perfect harmony with this organization, and neither dispenses with any of these powers nor violates them, in either the physical or the spiritual system.

10. The conclusion from the premises—that the constitution of the mind being the same after as before conversion—is that the process continues to be the same; that

the Spirit of God does not annihilate, metamorphose, or in any way circumvent any power or faculty of the mind in any of these effects upon the sinner or within the saint, and therefore performs these operations through the testimony of the truth and *through the Word of Truth alone.*

These summarized statements envelop the range of Campbell's teaching on Spiritual influence, as set forth in the Campbell-Rice Debate, and any references to the indwelling of the Spirit must be adapted to these postulations or it would serve only to array Campbell against Campbell.

Second: In the *Christian System,* under the chapter title, "Gift of the Holy Spirit," pages 48-49, there are three significant statements:

1. That we cannot separate the Spirit and the Word of God, and ascribe so much power to the one and so much to the other; for so did not the apostles. Whatever the Word does, the Spirit does; and whatever the Spirit does in the work of converting men, the Word does. We neither believe nor teach abstract Spirit nor abstract Word, but Word and Spirit, Spirit and Word.
2. That sanctification is unquestionably a progressive work; that to sanctify is to set apart; but there is a holy character as well as a holy state, and the formation of such a character is *the work of means: Sanctify them (the disciples) through thy truth; thy word is truth.*
3. That Christians are the temples of the Holy Spirit; and they are quickened, animated, encouraged, and sanctified by the power and influence of the Spirit of God, *working in them through the truth.*

Here is the crux of all that Campbell has said—that progressive sanctification in Christians is by the Holy Spirit working *through the truth.* Compare it with the statement in the first affirmative of the Campbell-Rice debate: If either conversion or sanctification is effected by the Word of Truth at all, it is by the Holy Spirit *through the Word alone.* Thus he affirmed the same *medium* for Spirit influence and operation to the sinner and to the saint.

Quoting the pioneers is treading on treacherous sands, besides being a poor way to prove anything. Already one of the *quoters* has printed an oblique apology for some misrepresentations by cautiously conceding that Lipscomb and Boles *felt* that the Spirit s indwelling was through the word. Shades of honesty! Why not state what they believed by quoting their *words* on the point without attempting a psychoanalysis of their supposedly re-pressed feelings on the subject.

In the writings of the early restorationists, including Stone and Campbell, are to be found repeated admissions of a gradual arrival at the whole truth on numerous points of theology, which accounts for contradictory pronouncements at different stages of this development. But we venture to aver that a poll of the pioneers in their maturity will not support the assertion that a majority of them held the view that the personal Holy Spirit dwells within a person *apart from* and *without* the Word. It is one thing to quote McGarvey and others on the indwelling Spirit, but it is something else to attach to their statements of that fact the added clause: *apart from, independent of, and without the Word of God.* The fragmentary quotations fall short of proving the point—that *one point* which is being so obviously and studiously avoided and ignored, namely, the *modus operandi:* the mode and the medium. Hearing a sermon preached on *The Power of the Word* is as scarce today as it was in sectarian denominational meetings in the past, yet that was the basic principle of the restoration plea as opposed to all mysterious operations in conversion and sanctification.

Chapter Three:
The Gift of the Holy Spirit

> *"Repent, and be baptized every one of you in the name of Jesus Christ for the remission of sins, and ye shall receive the gift of the Holy Spirit"*—Acts 2:38.

Much stress has been put on the genitive case of the phrase "the gift of the Holy Spirit" in the Greek text, and we are told that it is the *objective genitive* and must therefore mean that the personal Holy Spirit is the gift. But the genitive case in the Greek is the simple possessive in the English—and before clearing up this objective genitive *"irresponsible exegesis,"* a few simple observations with plain comparisons need to be noted.

First, the phrase "of the Holy Spirit" is in the possessive case. The use of the preposition 'of' before a noun in the English sentence makes it possessive. For example, *the farm of John Brown* is in the possessive case and means John Brown's farm. So in Acts 2:38 *the gift of the Holy Spirit* does not mean the Holy Spirit *as* a gift, but the Holy Spirit's gift.

Second, compare the following parallel phrases: (1) to the Samaritan woman Jesus said: "If thou knewest the gift of God... thou wouldst have asked him, and he would have given thee living water"—John 4:10; (2) to the Ephesians Paul said: "But unto every one of us is given grace according to the measure of the gift of Christ"—Eph. 4:7. Now, no one would even dare to say that *the gift of God* in John 4:10 is God himself; or that *the gift of Christ* in Eph. 4:7, is Christ himself; but the phrases in these passages are identical in the sentence structure with *the gift of the Holy Spirit* in Acts 2:38—yet they attempt to make the latter passage the Holy Spirit himself. The gift of God *does not* mean the *personal God;* the gift of Christ *does not* mean the *personal*

Christ—but the gift of the Holy Spirit, we are told, *does* mean the *personal Holy Spirit!* And with a flourish of the pen they write of *fallacy* in exegesis and illogical argument, in a supercilious criticism of others.

GIFT OF GOD—GIFT OF CHRIST—GIFT OF HOLY SPIRIT

Let us observe further by comparison the words and the structure of the phrases in these passages. The word *gift* in each of the passages is the Greek noun *dorea:* "The gift *(dorea)* of God"—John 4:10; "the gift *(dorea)* of Christ—Eph. 4:7; "the gift *(dorea)* of the Holy Spirit"—Acts 2:38: the same word, the same structure. The *gift of God* in John 4:10 to the Samaritan woman was God's gift to her—the living water. The *gift of Christ* in Eph. 4:7 to the Ephesians was Christ's gift to them—the blessings of the grace mentioned in the text. By the same simple syntax, in the plain grammar of it, the *gift of the Holy Spirit* in Acts 2:38 was the Holy Spirit's gift—"for the promise is unto you, and to your children, and to all that are afar off even as many as the Lord our God shall call." The Holy Spirit's gift was all that is included within this promise in all of its equivalent terms, the blessings of the Holy Spirit's dispensation for the Jew and the Gentile: "Unto you, and to your children, and to all that are afar off even as many as the Lord our God shall call."

Thus in the meaning of these passages, the *dorea* (gift) of God, and the *dorea* (gift) of Christ, and the *dorea* (gift) of the Holy Spirit, are all used in the special sense—specifying what God and Christ and the Holy Spirit are doing. The *dorea of God* in John 4:10 was that which proceeded from God, the living water; the *dorea of Christ* was that which proceeded from Christ—the measure of grace to each several member in the distribution of the spiritual endowments. On precisely the same premise the *dorea of the Holy Spirit* was that which proceeded from the Holy Spirit—the salvation and blessing of the all-inclusive promise mentioned without even a break in the context.

THE OBJECTIVE AND POSSESSIVE CASES

The argument based on an assertion that *the gift of the Holy Spirit* in Acts 2:38 is in the *objective genitive* case, and therefore the personal Holy Spirit must be the direct object of the verb 'receive,' requires some further attention. The late Doctor A.T. Robertson has been called the incomparable master and teacher of the New Testament Greek. His exhaustive *Grammar of the Greek New Testament* comprises nearly fifteen hundred pages. On pages 493 to 501 he discusses the relation of both the subjective and the objective cases to the possessive genitive, and clearly states that the possessive genitive may carry along with it either without changing the possessive structure of the sentence.

Now the *genitive* is the simple possessive, and it is the *specifying* case—as Robertson states, "it is this and no other"—it becomes the adjectival case, or a noun functioning as an adjective. For example "the gospel of John" is *John's gospel,* and the adjectival form makes the noun *John* an adjective, in its use. So in Acts 2:38 "the gift of the Holy Spirit" in the possessive genitive is of adjectival construction—hence, the *Holy Spirit's gift* takes the adjectival form and the noun *Holy Spirit* becomes an adjective in use as in the example of John's gospel—the Holy Spirit's gift.

On the subject of the subjective and the objective in relation to the possessive genitive the Robertson *Grammar of the Greek New Testament* says, on pages 499 to 501, that the subjective can be distinguished from the objective only by the context, and that in such instances the genitive remains the common possessive merely looked at from another angle. It further states, in itself the genitive is neither subjective nor objective, but lends itself readily to either point of view without changing the possessive case. This means, in the case of Acts 2:38, that "the gift of the Holy Spirit" is the possessive genitive—that is, *the Holy Spirit's gift*—but it embodies the objective in that which the Holy Spirit gives, or the gift that proceeds from the Holy Spirit, would be the far out object—thus the objective element reaches out beyond the possessive, but does not change the possessive case.

Thus the "objective genitive" argument of the professors falls flat, and the misuse of it in the attempt to force "the gift of the Holy Spirit" to mean a direct indwelling of the personal Holy Spirit is a failure. It is not the objective genitive—but is plainly the possessive case with the objective point of view, which is the Holy Spirit's gift, and in the adjectival form it is descriptive of what the Holy Spirit gives or bestows, or the blessings that proceed from it. This genitive, which in our English is the simple possessive, simply does what is termed expressing quality, as an adjective qualifies or describes the noun—and in this case the *Holy Spirit* is adjectival in its use, simply used as an adjective to qualify and describe the noun *gift*—the Holy Spirit's gift. These men are taking advantage of the readers and "by smooth and fair speech" they have beguiled the innocent, by making assertions about "the Greek genitive" which neither text nor *context in the Greek or in the English* will support.

THE OBJECT OF THE VERB 'RECEIVE'

In the study of Acts 2:38—"ye shall receive the gift of the Holy Spirit"—it is outside the range of grammatical structure to have the verb 'receive' governing both the accusative noun *gift* and the possessive genitive noun *of Spirit.* The accusative case is the object of verbs or prepositions; and the genitive is identical with the English possessive. In the sentence "ye shall receive the gift of the Holy Spirit," the verb *receive* is *lambano,* and the accusative noun *gift* is *dorean,* and the possessive genitive noun *of Spirit* is *Pneumatos:* Ye shall receive (lambano) the gift (dorean) of Spirit (Pneumatos). Now, the accusative noun *dorean* (gift) and the possessive genitive noun *Pneumatos* (of Spirit), because of their different case, cannot be the double objects after any verb. To make *gift,* the accusative (dorean), and *of Spirit,* the possessive genitive (Pneumatos), the objects of the one verb receive (lambano) is not grammatically possible.

For further illustration, "the gift of God" and "the gift of Christ" are definitely in the possessive genitives. So, the noun *gift* (accusative) and the phrase "of God" (possessive genitive), simply because one is the accusative case and the other the genitive possessive case, cannot be the objects of the same verb, *Greek or English.* But in Acts 2:38 the phrase "of Spirit" is the same structure, of the exact construction as "of God" and "of Christ"—the possessive genitive case. Now, the *gift of God* (John 4:10) and the *gift of Christ* (Eph. 4:7) and the *gift of the Holy Spirit* (Acts 2:38) are the same identical phrase. The noun *gift* is the accusative case and is the direct object; but "of God" and "of Christ" and "of the Holy Spirit" are all in the possessive case. Therefore, just as "the gift of God" means *God's gift,* and "the gift of Christ" means *Christ's gift,* so "the gift of the Holy Spirit" means the *Holy Spirit's gift.* The gift of God (John 4:10) , being in the possessive genitive, God himself cannot be the gift; and, the gift of Christ (Eph. 4:7), being the possessive genitive, Christ himself cannot be the gift—so, the gift of the Holy Spirit (Acts 2:38), being possessive genitive, the Holy Spirit himself cannot be the gift.

The *Young's Analytical Concordance* lists eleven passages in our New Testament where the noun *gift,* from dorea, occurs, followed by the possessive phrase—and in every instance it carries the meaning of what is given, or what proceeds from the source named. In Acts 8:20: "Thy silver perish with thee, because thou hast thought that *the gift of God* may be purchased with money"—here the gift was not God, but something that proceeded from God, an imparted power. In Rom. 5:17: "Much more they which receive abundance of grace and of *the gift of righteousness* shall reign in life by one, Jesus Christ"—here the gift is that which proceeds from righteousness (justification) in the life of the one reigning, or living with Christ. In Eph. 3:7: "According to *the gift of the grace of God"*—here the gift was what Paul had received from grace—what the grace of God had given to him as an apostle. All of these phrases are of the same construction, and carry the same possessive genitive meaning.

So again: The gift of God in John 4:10 was the living water; the gift of Christ in Eph. 4:7 was the measure of spiritual endowments bestowed on them; the gift of God in Acts 8:20 was the imparted power which proceeded from God that Simon coveted; the gift of righteousness in Rom. 5:17 is what proceeds from righteousness into the life; the gift of grace in Eph. 3:7 was what had been received by or from grace. And the gift of the Holy Spirit in Acts 2:38 is the promise of salvation to all mankind, to both the Jew and the Gentile, in all of its equivalent terms, in the Holy Spirit's dispensation.

ON THE FULFILLED PROMISE

This promise of Acts 2:38-39 is the same promise of Acts 13:26, 32: "Men and brethren, children of the stock of Abraham, and whosoever among you feareth God, to you is the word of this salvation sent.... and we declare unto you glad tidings, how that the promise which was made unto your fathers, God hath fulfilled the same unto us his children." It is the same promise of Gal. 3:14, 29: "That the blessing of Abraham might come upon the Gentiles, that we might receive the promise of the Spirit through faith... and if ye be Christ's then are ye Abrahams seed, and heirs according to the promise." It is equated with Acts 3:19, which runs parallel with Acts 2:38: "Repent ye therefore, and be converted, that your sins may be blotted out, when the times of refreshing shall come from the presence of the Lord." The relation of the words and phrases of these passages is synonymic—they are amplifications extending the description of the blessings included in the Holy Spirit's gift of Acts 2:38, and projecting and explaining the promise of verse 39, as a result of the whole. All of these passages together are a commentary on *the gift of the Holy Spirit* in Acts 2:38.

ON RECEIVING THE HOLY SPIRIT

If the apostle Peter by inspiration had intended to make the Holy Spirit the direct object of the verb receive he would not have put in the word *gift* at all; he would have put *Holy Spirit* in the accusative case; but instead inspiration put *Holy Spirit* in the genitive possessive case, and the noun *gift* in the accusative, thus making the noun *gift* the direct object of the verb *receive*: what gift was received?—the Holy Spirit's gift. But if the inspired apostle had intended to make the Holy Spirit the gift he would have said, "ye shall receive the Holy Spirit"—as in other passages where the Holy Spirit in the special endowments was the gift. In John 20:22, Jesus *breathed* on the disciples who were to be his apostles, and said: *Receive ye the Holy Spirit.* Here the Holy Spirit is the accusative and is the direct object of the verb *receive*. In Acts 19:2 Paul said to the twelve: Have ye received *the Holy Spirit* since ye believed.... and when Paul had laid hands upon them, the Holy Spirit came upon them." It is obvious that both of these instances were examples of the miraculous reception of the Holy Spirit which belonged only to the time of these special endowments. But the passages exemplify the difference in receiving the Holy Spirit and in receiving the gift of the Holy Spirit. Jesus did not say to the apostles: Receive ye the *gift of the Holy Spirit*—he said, Receive ye the *Holy Spirit;* and Paul did not say to the twelve: Have ye received *the gift of the Holy Spirit*—he said, Have you received *the Holy Spirit.* There is the difference and if the inspired apostle had intended to make *the Holy Spirit* the direct object of the verb receive in Acts 2:38, he would have put it that way, and the noun *Holy Spirit* would have been put in the accusative case, as a direct object. But the noun *gift* is the accusative case of that verse, and *of the Holy Spirit* is the genitive possessive, and it cannot be grammatically or scripturally applied any other way than "the Holy Spirit's gift"—in all of the amplifications of the promise of verse 39 and the equivalent terms of salvation, as a whole result, fulfilled to them on that Pentecost day and to us in the blessings of the gospel in the Holy Spirit's dispensation.

THE VIOLATION OF SYNTAX

The construction that has been placed upon Acts 2:38, to force the "gift of the Holy Spirit" to mean the direct indwelling of the personal Holy Spirit, violates the grammar of both the Greek and the English sentence, and all of the ado over the objective genitive case goes for naught. These men have imposed on readers of the various papers and magazines with assertions regarded by some of their readers as oracles, due to the positions they occupy as professors—but they are wrong, and when they are wrong, they are just as wrong as anybody, and usually more vulnerable.

The authorities on the New Testament Greek text herein cited are indisputably credible, and the ground on which these statements have been made is solid and subject to verification—and if necessary we can produce the whole sections in the authorities that deal with the cases that have been discussed which bear on the Acts 2:38 gift of the Holy Spirit.

But after all has been said, the one thing still remains. That one thing is the *modus operandi*—the medium of the Spirit's indwelling, for no matter how many verses may be cited to prove that the Spirit dwells in us, the whole question of medium remains and from this we shall not be drawn away—that the indwelling is only *through the Word.*

TODAY'S ENGLISH VERSION

The public has been treated to another blast of publicity for another new Bible—the *Today's English Version,* by the *American Bible Society.* In order to bolster his own exegesis of certain passages on the direct indwelling of the personal Holy Spirit, a professor hurried into print with an enthusiastic endorsement of this swaddling version, and cited Acts 2:38 among changes that "delighted" him. The *Today's* version renders Acts 2:38: "You shall receive God's Gift, the Holy Spirit." Now, anyone who knows anything about the Greek text, or who knows how to use just an Interlinear Greek-English New Testament, knows that there is no such phrase as "God's Gift, the Holy Spirit" in any of them. It is an arbitrary interpolation of a one-man so-called version of the New Testament, and it is a perversion.

An attempt has been made to defend the mistranslation of Acts 2:38 by this one-man version with a circular in which the statement was made that the word gift from the term *dorea* in the New Testament *always* means *God's gift.* If this is true then the word 'God' would necessarily be a part of the word dorea (gift) and must be translated to include it—but that is not true. Apply that erroneous statement to the passages that have been cited—John 4: 14 and Acts 8:20—where the phrase "the gift of God (dorea) would necessarily be translated *God's gift of God!* The professors who signed that circular made a stupid statement. If their assertion is true, the *one hundred forty-eight* translators—the most eminent and the ripest scholars of England and America, who translated our two old and time-tested versions—did not know it, for they followed no such idea. It is an indisputable fact that the phrase *the gift of God* in the passages cited is not God, but God's gift. And it is fully as undeniable that the phrase *the gift of the Holy Spirit* in Acts 2:38 is not the *Holy Spirit,* but *the Holy Spirit's* gift—which is everything included in verse 39, as has been previously proven, along with the fact that the one verb 'receive' cannot govern two different nouns in different cases as a double object. The noun *gift* in the objective case is the object of the verb *receive*, and *of the Holy Spirit* is in the possessive case, which makes the passage mean *the Holy Spirit's gift.* No other construction is consistent with both grammar and scripture, as has been fully sustained in the analysis of Acts 2:38 in foregoing sections of this treatise. These grammatical facts are unassailable.

A similar effort was made to defend the substitution of an entire clause, *turn away from your sins,* for the one word *repent.* That is not *translating*—it is *writing.* Another stupid statement was made that the word for *repent* always means *turn away from* in the New Testament. Then why is the ABS so inconsistent in translating it—for after changing it in Acts 2:38, the same word *repent* is left unchanged in Acts 3:19, and in other places. The word *metanoeo* for *repent* is used in this form thirty-four times in the New Testament, and means a change of mind or will—the mental act which precedes the turning, or reformation, which is the fruit of repentance mentioned in Matt. 3:8. This is a gospel truth, and these "scholarly" professors have confused *repentance* with *reformation,* which follows repentance—and the ABS so-called version is wrong again, as it is in multiplied examples—and the professors are going farther and farther from the truth in their efforts to defend these perversions.

The threadbare saying that *no translation is inspired* is a subterfuge behind which the promoters of these spurious versions now seek to hide. No person of right mind has ever objected to translation—the core of issue is the mistranslations, that these new bibles are not translations at all, but rather paraphrases, interpretations, and commentaries.

The *Septuagint* version of the Old Testament is a translation of the Hebrew Old Testament into the Greek. The Lord Jesus Christ and his inspired apostles quoted from the Septuagint Greek Old Testament—and they affirmed its inspiration. The Old Testament quotations in the New Testament are almost entirely from the Greek Old Testament—and if its inspiration was not lost in translation from the Hebrew, the whole issue turns on the *word-*

for-word translation of the Word of God—and that is the one thing the translators of the modern versions acknowledged that they have not done, and furthermore plainly stated that *they had no intention of so doing*! It is their own fatal admission that their books are not *the Bible* at all.

The diatribes that are now being hurled against the true and tested and tried Bible, produced by the one hundred and forty-eight of the greatest English and American scholars ever to be assembled, reminds all of us, who regard the Bible as the Word of God, of the carpings of the infidels against it in their age-long efforts to destroy it. As a mighty Gibraltar the Bible has withstood all such attacks from without, but the present onslaughts are from within—insidious and subtle—and far more dangerous. Our old Bible was produced in a generation of faith, whereas these modern pseudo-versions have been timed to a generation of doubt. It is a call to arms for the defense of the integrity of the Bible.

The internationally eminent Doctor Scott, of Northwestern University, who was the head of the Seminary of that institution, accused the translators of the *Revised Standard Version* of "deliberate dishonesty" and printed a long list of citations in his *Classical Weekly* in proof of his indictment. Doctor R.C. Foster, the ranking scholar of the Christian Church, who is head of their Seminary at Cincinnati, made a similar charge against the RSV translators in his series on "The Battle of the Versions" and cited multiple passages to prove his charge. But while these eminent educators were castigating the RSV for its perversions, our professors were endorsing and recommending it to the preachers, teachers, and churches. This is a disappointing thing, that we cannot look to our own educators to preserve the integrity of our Bible and to protect the church from the modernism of these versions—but *it is now apparent that we cannot do so.* This newly recommended *Today's English Version* falls under the same condemnation of deliberate mistranslation, and the young preachers, the young people, and the teachers of classes in the churches are simply being brainwashed in the acceptance of these far-out new versions.

Take a look at Rom. 1:17 in this new *Today's Version:* "For the gospel reveals how God puts man right with himself: it is through faith alone, from beginning to end." Will our professors be *delighted* with this "translation"—*through faith alone, from beginning to end*? Here is a serious question: How long will the people of the churches of Christ tolerate this sort of thing in our midst? The new translations that bear the titles *The New English Bible* and *The Revised Standard Version* are loaded with the same kinds of glaring and gross doctrinal errors, multiplied examples of which can be adduced. The men who are producing these new versions are Neo-Orthodox Modernists, and they are translating demons, engaged in the nefarious art of mutilating the Bible. Our young people and our young preachers are being brainwashed by these modern versions in college classes. What has gone wrong with the men of our colleges? There can be only one answer: *they are parroting the theologies* of the Seminaries where they received their Divinity degrees—and as a result we have some modern Bethanys developing in our brotherhood. After the death of Alexander Campbell the old Bethany College established by him fell to the Modernists, and now even the Conservative element of the Christian Church will not endorse it. Are we headed for another Bethany in Texas? The symptoms are unmistakably here.

Chapter Four:
The Special Gifts of the Holy Spirit

It is necessary to *dispensation* the Holy Spirit. The New Testament Church did not have the Word of God in the Book—it was in the revelation period, the Holy Spirit functioning stage. This is the evident meaning of 1 Cor. 14:6: "Now, brethren, if I come unto you speaking with tongues, what shall I profit you, except I shall speak to you either by revelation, or by knowledge, or by prophesying, or by doctrine." The province of the special gifts was specified in the four words: first, *revelation* was by direct inspiration; second, the *knowledge* that was imparted; third, the *prophecy* that was forth-telling rather than prophetical foretelling; fourth, the *doctrine* that was for instruction. These were all special spiritual endowments existing before "that which is perfect is come" of 1 Cor. 13, and which were to be done away. These were provisional gifts in the absence of the complete revelation of *the written word*. The mistake is now being made of taking these passages out of time and context.

THE TIME AND CONTEXT

It was clearly declared by the apostle in the 1 Cor. 14:6 passage that there could be no profit in the exercise of the gift of tongues, or of any of the special endowments, except for the purpose of completing divine revelation; therefore, there is no need, purpose, or reason for the existence of such gifts today. "Whether there be prophecies, they shall fail; whether there be tongues, they shall cease; whether there be knowledge, it shall vanish away. For we know in part, and we prophesy in part. But when that which is perfect is come, then that which is in part shall be done away"—1 Cor. 13:10. The mistake is now being made of taking these *spiritual gifts* passages out the time and context to which they belong.

This contextual consideration is the necessary approach to the Holy Spirit passages, without hedging or evasion, in the true context of each passage. It required special powers called *spiritual gifts* in bringing to completion the building that is called *the church.* These imparted gifts were the work of the Spirit expressed in the original word *charisma.* According to *Young's Analytical Concordance* this word is used in seventeen apostolic passages where the special gifts are indicated. There are only two exceptions, according to Young, where the reference to spiritual gifts does not come from charisma—1 Cor. 14:1 and 1 Cor. 14:12. In the first reference the apostle said: "Follow after charity, and desire spiritual *gifts."* Here the word *gifts* is in italics, showing that it was not in the original, but was the supplied word. The second reference reads: "Forasmuch as ye are zealous of spiritual *gifts."* And here again the word *gifts* is italicized. So the passages have the word *spiritual* without the word *gifts* in the original text: "Follow after charity, and desire spiritual *(pneumatika)";* and, "forasmuch as ye are zealous of spiritual (pneumaton"—literally, *of spirits).* In the translation *spiritual,* the gifts are necessarily implied and must be understood as meaning *spiritual things,* hence, spiritual gifts in the Corinthians 14 context. These are the only two places where the spiritual gifts are from the *pneuma* form of the word—in all of the other passages it is the word *charisma.* The reason for the mention of this is for emphasis—that the *charisma* gifts were all provisional, temporary, and were done away. And this is the word used in reference to the gifts mentioned in Rom. 12:6-8, 1 Cor. 12:1-11, and Eph. 4:8-16. In these verses, when the repetitions are cancelled, there are nineteen things listed among the *spiritual gifts* under the word *charisma.* The purpose of these *charisma* gifts was to impart the special powers to individual members, the number of persons necessary, as needed, in these various gifts for the edifying of the church in the absence of the completed revelation, the Word of God in *the written word.*

THE LAYING ON OF HANDS

These *charisma* gifts were *bestowed,* and for the specific limited period of the early church; and imparted by the laying on of the hands of the apostles; and only the apostles had this power of imparting these gifts to the several persons as required in the churches. The incident of Acts 8 is the proof of this fact; when the two apostles, Peter and John, were dispatched from Jerusalem to Samaria to impart the *spiritual gifts* where Philip the evangelist was baptizing many people. Though Philip himself possessed the *gifts,* and performed the miracles, he could not impart the gifts to others. So it was in the case of 1 Tim. 4:14: "Neglect not the gift that is in thee, which was given thee by prophecy, with the laying on of the hands of the presbytery." It is evident that the term *presbytery* here was a reference to Paul himself in the function that he performed in the laying of his hands on Timothy, mentioned in 2 Tim. 1:6; "That thou stir up the gift of God, which is in thee by the putting on of my hands." This affords the indisputable proof that by the ministration of the hands of Paul himself this gift was imparted to Timothy—therefore the hands of the presbytery in the first passage were the hands of Paul, the apostle. In all of these passages *charisma* had the *hands,* and when the last imparting hands left the world with the death of the last apostle, so did the source of these powers—the *charisma* gifts ceased with the last inspired man who could impart them.

THE RANGE OF IMPARTED GIFTS

For the readers who may desire to study these charisma references, they are as follows: Rom. 1:11; 11:29; 12:6; 1 Cor. 1:7; 1 Cor. 7:7; 1 Cor. 12:4,9,28,30,31; 2 Cor. 1:11; 1 Tim. 4:14; 2 Tim. 1:6; 1 Pet. 4:10. Within these fourteen passages is the whole range of the imparted gifts. In the other three verses—Rom. 5:15,

16; 6:23—the *charisma* was that one and only free-gift, the favor bestowed, the act of grace, that brought Christ from heaven into the world to complete the plan for salvation: "For the grace of God that bringeth salvation hath appeared to all men"—Tit. 2:11. In this act of grace, the free-gift bestowed and once given, completed and finished the scheme of redemption. "I have glorified thee on the earth: I have finished the work which thou gavest me to do"—John 17:4. The gift of God that sent Christ; the *paraclete* Comforter of inspiration given to the apostles of Christ; and the provisional charisma spiritual gifts imparted to the necessary number of members in the beginning period of the church of Christ, represented works that have been done, which require no repetition—the once-for-all things of the New Testament age that accomplished perfection of the church, the divine plan of salvation for man.

THE CESSATION OF PROVISIONAL GIFTS

Not having the written word to instruct them, it was necessary to possess these imparted special powers for the work of pastors, teachers, and evangelists. But it is reasonable that when the New Testament was completed these powers should be discontinued, as is plainly stated in 1 Cor. 13:8-10. These gifts were no longer needed. As it was in the creation of man, God said: "Let us make man in our image, after our likeness"—but when man was fully made in Adam, there was no need to continue the direct method used in forming him, and thereafter the natural law of procreation prevailed. So of the *new man,* the church—the special powers were necessary to form it, and in its growing stage, without the revealed word, the *charisma* gifts were indispensable. But as with Adam the creative powers were succeeded by natural law; so with the church, the new man, *revelation has been written down,* and the provisional gifts have been succeeded by the spiritual law. The word *gift* and *gifts* in other forms of the original terms occur thirty-eight times in the New Testament, but *charisma* is the word that designates the special spiritual gifts imparted by the laying on of hands. And the reason why the laying on of hands ceased, by which the special gifts were imparted, is because the things given ceased—that is, the *charisma* ceased with the last inspired man who could impart the gifts.

Chapter Five:
An Exposition of the Holy Spirit Passages

We come now to the examination of the passages that have been applied to the direct indwelling of "the personal Holy Spirit," and propose to prove that they have all been misapplied—that every passage so used has been misused.

In the first place, the monotonous repetition that "the personal Holy Spirit dwells in us" is not pertinent—the personality of the Holy Spirit has not been disputed. The point at issue is—does the Holy Spirit dwell within us personally. We all believe in the personal God and the personal Christ, but it has been conceded that neither God nor Christ dwells within us personally. So why the adroitness in shuffling the phraseology in reference to the indwelling of the Spirit, if not for the means of gaining an end. The adverb *personally* has been cleverly shifted to the adjective *personal* and transposed to the wrong end of the declarative sentence: the precise point is—*does the Spirit inhabit us personally?* In the second place, the misused passages fall short of the proof for which they have been adduced, inasmuch as each and every one has only stated *the fact* of the Spirit's indwelling, without indicating *the medium,* and the personal inhabitation of the Spirit has been arbitrarily assumed.

JOHN 7:38-39

> "*He that believeth on me, as the Scripture hath said, out of his belly shall flow rivers of living water. (But this spake he of the Spirit, which they that believe on him should receive: for the Holy Spirit was not yet given; because that Jesus was not yet*

glorified)."

The fact that John connected this promise of the Holy Spirit with the ascension of Christ makes it evident that the passage refers to the opening of the Holy Spirit's dispensation, and pointed to Pentecost. A companion reference is in Acts 5:32: "And we are his witnesses of these things; and so is also the Holy Spirit, whom God hath given to them that obey him." The statement in John pointed *forward* to the coming of the Spirit on Pentecost which they *should receive* (future), and the statement in Acts *pointed back* to the coming of the Spirit on Pentecost which God had given (past). In the Acts 5:32 passage it states that the apostles were *witnesses* of the *things* of which they testified, then adds: 'and so is also the Holy Spirit.' That is, the miraculous power of the Spirit given to them was the witness to the proof of what they were preaching. This fact is further stated in Heb. 2:4: "God also bearing them witness, both with signs and wonders, and with divers miracles, and gifts of the Holy Spirit, according to his own will." The phrase "according to his own will" in reference to these gifts of the Spirit make it plain that the passages apply to the gifts that were special, not general, and the distribution was based on the existing needs, hence, *according to his will*—that is, a special and not a general distribution—for the purpose of *bearing witness* to the preaching of the believers.

These passages are of the same import as the statement of Mark 16:16-20: "And these signs shall follow them that believe.... and they went forth, and preached everywhere, the Lord working with them, and confirming the word with the signs that followed." These references apply to the witness of the Holy Spirit to the preaching of the believers, in "signs and wonders, and with divers miracles, and gifts of the Holy Spirit" to confirm the Word preached by the apostles and the believers.

OPERATION VERSUS PERSONAL INDWELLING

In complete harmony with the foregoing, the statement of John 7:39 marks an operation, a manifestation, rather than personal indwelling. On this point the comments in the F.C. Cooke original Speaker's Bible Commentary are worthy of quotation. This valuable work was the result of a bill introduced in the English Parliament, by the Speaker of the House of Commons, to provide the funds for the publication of a commentary on the whole Bible by the scholars of England—and for that reason it was published under the title *The Speaker's Commentary*. On the reference to the Spirit in John 7:39, the following comments were made:

> "The Holy Ghost (Spirit) was not yet given. The addition of the word 'given' expresses the true form of the original, in which *Spirit* is without the article (the). When the term occurs in this form, it marks an operation, or manifestation, or gift of the Spirit, and not the personal Spirit."

That is the exact truth in regard to the Holy Spirit in John 7:38-39.

THE DIVINE MANIFESTATION

The *Shekinah* in the Old Testament—from the Hebrew word *shaken*, in such notable passages as Ex. 25:8; or *shakan*, Psa. 68:18—was the Divine Manifestation of God's earthly presence among the people, by which his presence was known to men. So the descent of the Spirit on Pentecost and the continued miraculous powers displayed were the Divine Manifestations of God's presence among the apostles and the believers of the new dispensation. These Old Testament *Shekinah* passages are quoted in the New Testament to exemplify God's presence and dwelling among his people in the new church. It is remarkable that the passage on gifts of the Spirit in Eph. 4:8 is quoted from Psa.

68:18. Read them side by side: "Thou has ascended on high, thou hast led captivity captive: thou hast received gifts for men; yea for the rebellious also, that the Lord God might dwell among them—Psa. 68:18. Now read Eph. 4:8: "Wherefore he saith, When he ascended on high, he led captivity captive, and gave gifts unto men." The word *dwell* in Psa. 68:18 is the word *shakan,* the Shekinah, or manifestation of God's presence, and in the New Testament the special *gifts* of Eph. 4:8, quoted from the Psalms text, were as the *Shekinah*—the miraculous Divine Manifestation of God's presence in the church of the new dispensation. These *gifts* in Psa. 68:18 and Eph. 4:8 were connected with the ascension of Christ "up on high" where he was glorified. In reference to precisely the same thing the John 7:39 passage applies to the ascension of Christ: "But this spake he of the Spirit, which they that believe on him should receive: for the Holy Spirit was not yet given; because that Jesus was not yet glorified." These parallels are the positive proof that the giving and receiving of the Spirit in John 7:39 referred to the special gifts of Eph. 4:8 as divine manifestations and not to the personal Holy Spirit indwelling as it has been forced to mean. Any professor who does not know how to *dispensation* the Holy Spirit passages of the New Testament is not qualified to prepare young men for the preeminent work of preaching the gospel to the people.

RIVERS OF LIVING WATER

But there are some further necessary observations on John 7:38-39 in reference to "the rivers of living water" which should flow from the believers after the Spirit was given. In John 4:14, Jesus said: "But whosoever drinketh of the water that I shall give him shall never thirst; but the *water* that I shall give him shall be in him a well of water springing up into everlasting life." Now, the two passages are on the same theme—beginning with verse 37 of the John 7 passage, Jesus said: "If any man thirst, let him come unto me and drink. He that believeth on me, as the Scripture hath said, out of his belly shall flow rivers of living water." Reading these passages side by side, the phrase *rivers of living water* is equated with a *well of water springing up*. The rivers of this living water would flow *out of* the believer and the well of water would *spring up in him*—the obvious meaning of which is that the salvation of the gospel should soon begin to flow in perennial stream through the believers. In the same connection, in chapter 6, Jesus said; "I am the bread of life: he that cometh to me shall never hunger; and he that believeth on me shall never thirst and they shall be all taught of God. Every man therefore that hath heard, and hath learned of the Father, cometh unto me.... I am the living bread which came down out of heaven: if any man eat of this bread, he shall live forever." It should not be difficult for anyone to see that flowing rivers, the springing well, and the living bread were the blessings that would proceed from the Spirit through the teaching—every man who was taught, who had *heard* and *learned* and who would thus *come* entered into the blessings of the flowing rivers and the springing well of salvation's unceasing stream of spiritual life-giving waters.

THE HOLY SPIRIT'S TRUTH

The casual connection in all of these verses is the *Spirit's Truth,* in metaphors of *living water* and *living bread—to eat* and *drink* the *truth* which Jesus taught. It is the word that runs through John's gospel—it begins with the word *truth* and ends with the word *truth:* Jesus was "full of grace and truth"—1:14; "grace and truth came by Jesus Christ"—3:21; the "witness of the truth"—5:33; you shall "know the truth, and the truth shall make you free"—8:32; and Jesus declared himself to be "the way, the truth, and the life—14:6—and prayed that his disciples should be sanctified "through thy truth: thy word is truth"—17:17.

These are a few of the twenty-eight times that *the truth* is mentioned in the gospel of John. The *Spirit's Truth* is the shrine of the Spirit's power, and it is made potential to man by faith, which makes the heart the well-spring of life. The *Spirit's Truth* is the pabulum on which the soul feeds, and in the ratio of the truth assimilated in the germinal process, through the bioplasts of the soul, it is woven into the tissue and the fibre of the inner man. The *Spirit's Truth* is therefore the answer to spiritual life and all of its outflowings in the rivers of the water of life: "For from you sounded out the word of the Lord"—and this sounding out of the Word of Truth is the flowing out of all the believers of the rivers of water and the well of water which imparts the everlasting life. This is how the Holy Spirit in John 7:39, which was not yet given, should be the source of the flowing there mentioned—the *truth* is the medium.

LUKE 11:13

> *"If ye then, being evil, know how to give good gifts unto your children: how much more shall your heavenly Father give the Holy Spirit to them that ask him?"*

This passage is in the context of Luke's record of the *Sermon on the Mount.* The parallel passage in Matthew's account reads: "How much more shall your Father which is in heaven give good things to them that ask him?' Here is an equation: the *Holy Spirit* in Luke is equated with *good things* in Matthew. It is another example of metonymy—the use of a term in the place of another: the Holy Spirit is put for the *things* of the Spirit, that which proceeds from the Spirit, and it means the *spiritual teaching* in the gospel. The teaching of Christ in all of these statements was dispensational—pointing to Pentecost and the beginning of the approaching gospel dispensation.

The Holy Spirit does not enter anyone through prayer, but through the teaching of the Spirit: "For by one Spirit are we all baptized into one body, whether we be Jews or Gentiles, whether we be bond or free, and have all been made to drink into one

Spirit"—1 Cor. 12:13. It is by the agency of the Spirit through teaching that we are baptized into one body, the church, where we drink into the Spirit by participating in its blessings. And the teaching of Christ from his baptism in the Jordan to his death on the cross pointed to the Holy Spirit's dispensation with all of its gospel blessings.

ASKING AND RECEIVING
The context of Luke 11:13 is connected with the immediate preceding verses: "And I say unto you, Ask, and it shall be given you; seek and ye shall find; knock and it shall be opened unto you. For every one that asketh receiveth; and he that seeketh flndeth; and to him that knocketh it shall be opened." These verses form the premises for the Lord's admonition concerning asking for the good things of the Holy Spirit which he had announced in the good glad news of the gospel, soon to be proclaimed in the approaching dispensation.

In the grammar of the text the verb *ask* is the present imperative, which indicates continuing desire—it is not a reference to prayer or praying, but the desiring that becomes a part of the inner being.

ASKING AND CALLING
The corresponding text of Rom. 10:13-17 is a definition of what it means to ask, and knock, and seek:

> *"Whosoever shall call upon the name of the Lord shall be saved. How then shall they call on him in whom they have not believed? And how shall they believe in him of whom they have not heard? And how shall they hear without a preacher? And how shall they preach except they be sent? As it is written, How beautiful are the feet of them that preach the gospel of peace, and bring glad tidings of good things! But they have not all*

> *obeyed the gospel. For Isaiah saith, Lord, who hath believed our report. So then faith cometh by hearing, and hearing by the word of God."*

These verses describe the sending of the apostles of Christ to preach the good things of salvation in the gospel. All who call, in this Romans passage, correspond to the ones who ask, in the Luke passage. But the calling on the name of the Lord in Rom. 10:13 is obeying the gospel of verse 16—and the asking of Luke 11:13 is the same thing as the *calling* in Rom. 10:13, and it, has no reference to "praying for the personal Holy Spirit to enter into us." The comparisons are here made out: Asking is calling, and calling is hearing, believing, and obeying. Asking does not refer to praying and pleading, and knocking at the door does not mean knocking the door down!

The one who hears the gospel is the seeker; the one who believes the gospel is the knocker; and the one who obeys the gospel is the finder—and the asker is all of them, and he receives that which he asked. It all points to Pentecost, where its connection with the gospel is the equivalence of asking the question, "Men and brethren, what shall we do?" The answer was that upon repentance and baptism for the remission of sins they should receive the gift of the Holy Spirit in all of the equivalent terms of salvation. Therefore, the promise of the Holy Spirit in Luke 11:13 was dispensational and was equated with the *good things* of the Spirit in the blessings of the gospel.

ACTS 2:1-4

> *"And when the day of Pentecost was fully come, they were all with one accord in one place. And suddenly there came a sound from heaven as of a rushing of a mighty wind, and it filled all the house where they were sitting. And there appeared unto them cloven tongues like as of fire, and it sat*

> *upon each of them. And they were all filled with the Holy Spirit, and began to speak with other tongues, as the Spirit gave them utterance."*

To further enforce the direct indwelling of the Spirit, the attempt has been made to include all the believers on that Pentecost day in the statement: "And they were all filled with the Holy Spirit." Most of our preachers and the brethren generally have long known that only the apostles were the recipients of the Holy Spirit baptism on Pentecost, but now our sophistic professors would have *all the believers* included in the declaration "they were all filled with the Holy Spirit."

THE ANTECEDENT OF THE PRONOUN

It is elementary that the antecedent of the pronoun *they* in the first verse of the second chapter of Acts is *the eleven apostles* (increased to twelve) mentioned in the preceding last verse of the first chapter: "And they gave forth their lots; and the lot fell upon Matthias; and he was numbered with the eleven apostles. And when the day of Pentecost was fully come *they* were all of one accord in one place... and *they* were all filled with the Holy Spirit." Grammatically connecting these two verses, without a break in the context, makes the *apostles* (the eleven and Matthias) the antecedent of the pronoun *they* in Acts 2:1, and *them* in verse 3, and *they* again in verse 5—adding to these, verse 14, that "Peter stood up with the eleven." Since the name of McGarvey has been so repeatedly appropriated by these men, let them hear him on this point:

> "The persons thus assembled together and filled with the Holy Spirit were not, as many have supposed, the one hundred and twenty disciples mentioned in a parenthesis in the previous chapter, but the twelve apostles. This is made certain by the grammatical connection between the first verse of this chapter

and the last of the preceding. Taken together they read as follows: 'And they gave lots for them, and the lot fell upon Matthias; and he was numbered with the eleven apostles. And when the day of Pentecost was now come, they were all together in one place'. The house in which the apostles were sitting was not the upper chamber in which they were abiding, but some apartment of the temple; for, as we learn from Luke's former treatise, the apostles during these days of waiting were 'continually in the temple praising God'; that is, continually there through the hours in which the temple was open. The upper chamber was their place of lodging."

THE AUDACITY OF THE NEW VERSION

But now our pragmatic professors have summoned to their aid the latest new translation of the New Testament—*Today's English Version,* the one-man translation published by the American Bible society, in which the pronoun *they* in Acts 2:1 is made to read *all the believers.* But the word *they* is a pronoun, the word *all* is an adjective, and the word *believers* is a noun—and this so-called version has substituted an adjective and a noun, which are not in the text at all, for a pronoun which is in the text! Yet they would call that *translation*, and a pedantic professor in our college endorsed and recommended it! Such a thing as that is not *translating* the New Testament, it is *writing* one! It is a violation of the grammatical construction of Acts 2:1 and a completely unwarranted deviation from the text and its teaching.

ACTS 2:38—ACTS 3:19

"Repent, and be baptized every one of you in the name of Jesus Christ for the remission of sins, and ye shall receive the gift of the Holy Spirit"

> *"Repent ye therefore, and be converted, that your sins may be blotted out, when the times of refreshing shall come from the presence of the Lord."*

Now, the American Bible Society version has substituted the word *turn* for *repent* in Acts 2:38—but left the word *repent* in Acts 3:19, though it is the same word in both places in the original text. Why this difference? Simply because it served a purpose to change it. Obviously, the word *turn* could not be put in place of the word *repent* in Acts 3:19, for *be converted* is the turning in that passage.

Neither faith nor repentance is turning. In Acts 11:22, it is said that "many believed and turned"—so faith was not the turning act, for they believed and turned. In Acts 3:19, it reads "repent and (turn) be converted"—so repentance is not the turning act, for they were commanded to *repent and turn.* But comparing Acts 2:38 with Acts 3:19: first, *repent and be baptized;* second, *repent and be converted.* So what the command to *be baptized* means in Acts 2:38, the command to *be converted* means in Acts 3:19—so the turning act is *be baptized,* or *be converted.* There is no reason for changing the word repent in one passage and leaving the same word unchanged in the other passage—it is arbitrary translation, or simply no translation.

OTHER DEVIATIONS FROM THE TEXT

Another example of the same deviation from the text by this American Bible Society translation is in Acts 8:20. The passage reads "thy silver perish with thee"—but the new *Today's Version* has the apostle to tell Simon to *go to hell,* thus joining the Phillip's Translation which reads: "To hell with you and your money!" Here these versions have translated the verb *perish* into the noun *hell.* The word *perish* is the verb *apollumi,* and it is mistranslated into the noun *hell*—but there is no word at all for *hell* in the text. These men got smart with language and revealed their vindictive translation policies in a crude style that reflects on the apostle Peter as employing a manner of street cursing. It is wicked to make such degrading translations—these new translators are theological demons.

It has been shown also that the translation of the phrase "gift of the Holy Spirit" in Acts 2:38 into *God's gift, the Holy Spirit* eliminates the prepositional phrase *of the Holy Spirit* and changes the whole structure of the sentence—and there is no word in the text at all from which *God's gift* could be derived. The recent recommendation of this *Today's Version* by our professors reveals a lack of wise and accurate scholarship, as well as too little respect for the original text of God's Word.

THE EQUATION OF THE TWO PASSAGES

This brings us to the equation of Acts 2:38 and Acts 3: 19: Both passages have the word *repent;* one has *be baptized,* and the other *be converted;* one has *for the remission of sins,* and the other sins *blotted out;* one has the *gift of the Holy Spirit,* and the other *times of refreshing from the presence of the Lord.* Here the command to be baptized is equated with the command to be converted; and the *remission of sins* is equated with *sins blotted out;* and the *gift of the Holy Spirit* is equated with *times of refreshing*—what the one is in all of these phrases, so is the other, and they are equations, they are parallel. The expression "when the times of refreshing shall come from the presence of the Lord" referred to the blessings of the gospel dispensation and the *when* meant that when they obeyed the command to repent and be converted they would come into blessings embodied therein. So the expression *shall receive the gift of the Holy Spirit* meant: when they obeyed the command to repent and be baptized they would come into the promised blessings in all of its equivalent terms of salvation. The *when* of the one is the *when* of the other, and the meaning is no more and no less—and the gift of the Holy Spirit in Acts 2:38 is equated with the blessings of the Holy Spirit's dispensation in Acts 3: 19.

RECEIVING THE WORD AND THE SPIRIT

A dodge hardly worth the notice has been attempted by connecting Acts 2:38 with the following verse 41, which reads: "Then they that gladly received his word were baptized"—and we are told that if receiving the word is receiving the Spirit, then they received the Spirit before they were baptized! Only a tyro could emit such sophistry. The word in verse 41 where they gladly received the word, is *apodechomi* which means to welcome, but in verse 38 "shall receive the gift" is *lambano* which means *to take.* Another example of the use of the first word and its meaning is in Luke 8:40, where the people *gladly received* Jesus—they welcomed him—the same word as in Acts 2:41. But another example of the second word is in Gal. 3:2, where the Galatians received the Spirit through the hearing of faith—and that is the same word as in Acts 2:38. Of course, the *Word* is not the Spirit, but it is the medium through which the Spirit operates upon and dwells within us, therefore the medium of reception.

After all has been said on Acts 2:38 from any worthy pen, McGarvey's or any other, that the gift of the Spirit means the Holy Spirit "as a gift," the quotations still fall short of proving the assertion that it is received or dwells within us apart from the word. But we have previously shown that the phrase *the gift of God* in John 4:14, and the phrase *the gift of Christ* in Eph. 4:7, and *the gift of the Holy Spirit* in Acts 2:38, are all in the possessive case—God's gift was the living water; Christ's gift was the measure of grace mentioned; and the Holy Spirit's gift was all that the promise included in all the equivalent terms of salvation.

ACTS 5:32

> *"And we are witnesses of these things; and so is also the Holy Spirit, whom God hath given to them*

that obey him."

The use of the word *witnesses* in this passage connects the Holy Spirit with the miraculous powers employed by the apostles of Christ in demonstration of the truth which was preached by them. It also connects this passage with Heb. 2:4: "God also bearing them witness, both with signs and wonders, and with divers miracles, and gifts of the Holy Spirit, according to his own will." These gifts of the Holy Spirit were distributed *according to his will,* that is, as they were needed and required; and they were for the purpose of bearing witness to the truth. The fact that Heb. 2:4 is a reference to Mark 16:17-20 makes it evident that these verses all apply to the special powers of the Holy Spirit in the believers: "These signs shall follow them that believe.... and they went forth, and preached everywhere, the Lord working with them, and confirming the word with signs following." The passage of Acts 5:32 clearly states that the Holy Spirit was there given to witness the preaching of the apostles, and therefore referred to the miraculous powers and not to a personal Holy Spirit indwelling. For further discussion of the Acts 5:32 text, refer to the discussion of John 7:38-39 and Luke 11:13.

ACTS 19:1-6

"It came to pass, that while Apollos was at Corinth, Paul having passed through the upper coasts came to Ephesus; and finding certain disciples, he said unto them, Have ye received the Holy Spirit since ye believed? And they said unto him, We have not so much as heard whether there be any Holy Spirit. And he said unto them, Unto what then were be baptized? And they said, Unto John's baptism. Then said Paul, John verily baptized with the baptism of repentance, saying unto the people, that they should believe on him which should come

after him, that is, on Christ Jesus. When they heard this, they were baptized in the name of the Lord Jesus. And when Paul had laid his hands upon them, the Holy Spirit came on them; and they spake with tongues, and prophesied."

it is so evident here as to be certain that the reception of the Holy Spirit mentioned by Paul in this text was in reference to the impartation of spiritual gifts by the hand of an apostle—which Paul meant to bestow on them, as indicated by the fact that he did so, as stated in verse 6—it could not have referred to the promise of Acts 2:38 to all baptized believers, for such a question would have been useless, forasmuch as all the baptized do receive that blessing. This passage therefore refers to the Spiritual Gifts endowments, and cannot be applied to the believers today.

THE IMPARTED POWERS
This fact is made further evident by Paul's question to the twelve—"have ye received the Holy Spirit since ye believed?" The apostle did not ask if they had received *the gift of the Holy Spirit* in the phrase of Acts 2:38—but have ye received *the Holy Spirit,* and here it referred to the imparted powers received only through the laying on of the hands of the apostles: "And when Paul had laid hands upon them, the Holy Spirit came upon them." The men who are teaching the direct operations and indwelling of the Holy Spirit today are not *dispensationing* the Holy Spirit, and are repeating the mistakes and blunders of the denominational clergy through all time since the origination of their doctrines of inherent sin, direct operation of the Holy Spirit, and the impossibility of apostasy—they all go together, and they stand or fall together.

And now comes the suggestion that we change the name of the *Acts of the Apostles* to the title: *The Acts of the Holy Spirit!* In that case, why not also change the names of the epistles to *The*

Epistles of the Holy Spirit. What is the motive? In Luke's record of the Great Commission, Jesus said to his apostles: "Ye are witnesses of these things." And in Acts 1:8: "And ye shall be witnesses unto me." And after becoming an apostle Paul was made a witness, as related in Acts 22:16: "For thou shalt be his witness unto all men." These words of Jesus to his apostles make the book of Acts, *The Acts of the Apostles,* and it bears the right title. It is evident that there are men among us in high places who are bent on changing the Bible and the church, and that an unsavory movement is in motion in our great and growing brotherhood.

ROMANS 5:5

> *"And hope maketh not ashamed; because the love of God is shed abroad in our hearts by the Holy Spirit which is given unto us."*

It is significant that Berry's Interlinear Greek-English text in the original reads: the love of God *has been shed* (poured out)—by the Holy Spirit which was given to us; and it is the *aorist* tense of absolute past, which connects Rom. 5:5 with Acts 2:33: "He hath shed forth this which ye now see and hear." It points back to the miraculous work of the Holy Spirit on Pentecost, functioning in the revelation of the love of God, which has been shed *by the agency of the Spirit* in the hearts of all who accept it. It has the same significance as Tit. 3:6, "which he shed on us abundantly," an obvious reference to the miraculous powers of the Holy Spirit in the dispensation of the special gifts. The *aorist* past tense of Rom. 5:5 makes it refer to a thing that had been done and, together with Tit. 3:6, it is another dispensational passage that reverts to Pentecost, to the Holy Spirit's function in bringing to us the love of God through the revelation of the gospel.

It is claimed that God's love is diffused in the heart by the direct indwelling of "the personal Holy Spirit." But it is said in Tit. 3:5-6 that the Holy Spirit "is shed on US abundantly through (by)

Jesus Christ." So here is a comparison: if the phrase "by the Holy Spirit" in Rom. 5:5 means the direct indwelling of the personal Holy Spirit, then the phrase "through (or by) Jesus Christ" in Tit. 3:6 would mean the direct indwelling of the personal Christ. But they have conceded that the personal Christ does not dwell in us. Yet the prepositional phrases in these two passages are exactly the same. Both prepositions, *by* and *through,* are translated from the one preposition *dia* in the text, and both followed by the genitive, according to Bagster's lexical Greek Concordance and Young's Analytical Concordance—and the meaning of the preposition in both passages is *through, by means of.* So if the shedding of the Holy Spirit on us by Jesus Christ does not mean the direct indwelling of the personal Christ, then the shedding of the love of God in us by the Holy Spirit does not mean the direct indwelling of the personal Holy Spirit. The prepositional phrases simply denote the agency of the Holy Spirit, and the expressions *shed abroad in our hearts* and *shed on us abundantly* mean that the revelation of the gospel, attested by miraculous powers and spiritual gifts, had filled their heart with the knowledge of the love of God.

THE LIGHT AND IMAGE OF GOD

In 2 Cor. 4:4-6 Paul proceeds further to say that God "hath shined in our hearts" the light of the gospel. The love of God of Rom. 5:5, is "shed abroad in our hearts by the Holy Spirit" in the same way that the light and image of God, of 2 Cor. 4:4-6, "hath shined in our hearts" by the glorious gospel. The same process is expressed in different words, but convey the same idea, and state the same thing. The *how* that the light and image of God is *shined* in the heart by the glorious gospel is the exact *how* that the love of God is shed in the heart by the Holy Spirit.

There is no cognition of the love of God apart from the Word of God. The source of this cognizance is by the Holy Spirit as the agent. It is connected with identifying the things which the Word of God has promised. The heart through the mind or intellect understands what the Word has promised, and our consciences respond as we know and recognize it. The phrase *by the Holy Spirit* simply expresses agency—the Holy Spirit revealed the love of God and we are conscious of its influence through the Word. There were direct manifestations and special gifts *then* but it is *through the written word* embraced by the soul now that the Holy Spirit bears witness of the love of God to the child of God, and thus sheds abroad or diffuses the love of God in our hearts.

ROMANS 8:9-26

The references to the Spirit in Romans the eighth chapter have three applications: First, the spirit, mind, and disposition of Christ; second, the spirit of adoption and sonship as contrasted with the spirit of the slave or servant; third, one's own spirit, the human spirit.

In chapter 8, verse 9, the expression "the Spirit of God" and "the Spirit of Christ" are interchangeable, and the clause" if any man have not the Spirit of Christ, he is none of his" is followed by the phrase, in verse 10, "and if Christ be in you." This is Paul's own commentary that the indwelling of the Spirit means the same thing as "Christ in you"—and the one can be no more personal than the other. The verses that refer to the witness of the Spirit apply to rendering service to God as sons of God, and not as slaves; and the spirit of sonship in which we serve God agrees with the witness or testimony of the Holy Spirit regarding our sonship. In verses 26 and 27 the apostle refers to the intercession of the Spirit on our behalf "with groanings which cannot be uttered," and it has been urged that this is something the Holy Spirit does which is not ascribed to the Word. But the exception is not valid, for the reference here would describe the Spirit's influence upon God in heaven, not upon us. It was suggested to me years ago by R.L. Whiteside, that the Spirit in Romans 8:26-27 refers to the human spirit and not to the Holy Spirit, and the meaning of the text, therefore, is that our own spirit groans or yearns in intercession to God for that which cannot be uttered, or put into words.

The passage refers to the groaning of the spirit. But why should the Holy Spirit groan? Groaning is indicative of pain—the Holy Spirit is not in pain—but our own spirit groans within us when we are unable to utter in words, to make vocal, our yearnings, "for we know not what we should pray for as we ought." But in heaven "he that searches the hearts knoweth what is the mind of the spirit"—our spirit—which groans in the inability to put in words its yearnings, and it thus makes intercession for us, for God knows its mind.

The fact that the word Spirit in the text has the capital *S* does not prove it to be the Holy Spirit, for in our first printed scriptures all of the letters were capitals; and there are numerous other verses in Romans 8, and other chapters, where the word spirit has the capital *S,* but where the text and the context clearly indicate the human spirit, mind, or disposition.

But granting that the passage refers to the intercession of the Holy Spirit, the passage does not refer to any action of the Holy Spirit upon or in us and therefore does not offer an exception to the proposition that every influence upon us that the Bible ascribes to the Holy Spirit, it also affirms of the Word of God. This does not minimize the Holy Spirit, it magnifies the Word of God. The exertion to adapt the eighth chapter of Romans to the direct indwelling of "the personal Holy Spirit" violates the whole context of the chapter.

> *Verses 9-10: "But we are not in the flesh, but in the Spirit, if so be that the Spirit of God dwells in you. Now if any man have not the Spirit of Christ, he is none of his. And if Christ be in you, the body of sin is dead because of sin, but the Spirit is life because of righteousness."*

1. The phrase *in the Spirit* put in contrast with *in the flesh* obviously refers to the human spirit. It would be sheer tautology to say if the Holy Spirit dwells in us we are in the spirit! So the contrast is between the flesh and the spirit of man.

2. The Spirit of God and the Spirit of Christ dwelling in you, of verse 9, are the same thing.

3. The Spirit in you and Christ in you, of verse 10, are the same indwelling—which means that the Spirit dwells in us the same way that Christ dwells in us. It is not claimed that the personal Christ dwells in us—and on the basis of verses 9 and 10 it cannot be consistently claimed that the personal Holy Spirit dwells in us.

From other passages it is plain that Christ dwells in us when the character of Christ is formed within us, as stated in Gal. 4:19. The Holy Spirit dwells in us in the same way that Christ is formed in us. But the personal Christ is not formed in us, and for the same reason the personal Holy Spirit does not dwell in us. Christ lives in us "by the faith of the Son of God" (Gal. 2:20), and the Holy Spirit dwells in us in the same way that Christ lives in us, according to verses 9 and 10: "If any man have not the Spirit of Christ... And if Christ be in you"—the Spirit of Christ in you is here equated with Christ in you, and therefore refers to the mind, the disposition, and the character of Christ which the Spirit imparts through his teaching.

> *Verses 14-16: "For as many as are led by the Spirit of God, they are the sons of God. For ye have not received the spirit of bondage again to fear; but ye have received the Spirit of adoption, whereby we cry, Abba, Father. The Spirit itself beareth witness with our spirit, that we are the children of God."*

1. To be led *by the Spirit* means to be guided, and the leading

of the Spirit is not an occult leading beyond the scope of understanding the truth, but rather the leading that is through the motives of the gospel, the Word of Truth. The premise of the Roman epistle was the power of the gospel, beginning with chapter one, and all of these conclusions proceed from it and are drawn from it. The Holy Spirit reveals to us in the gospel how to live in righteousness and in that way we are led by the Spirit.

2. The witness of the Spirit is through the testimony which the Spirit bears through his teaching. In verse 16, our own spirit is one of two witnesses: The Holy Spirit teaches that we are sons of God and not slaves—and the witness of our own spirit is joined with that of the Holy Spirit in the service rendered to God in the spirit of sons—the disposition or the attitude of sons—in which we serve the Father. Admittedly, the *spirit of bondage* and the *spirit of adoption,* as mentioned in verse 15, are not persons or beings but dispositions and attitudes of mind. So in the same context the reference to "our spirit" means the spirit of sonship. The first witness of these verses is the Holy Spirit's teaching that bears witness to our sonship (that we are children and heirs); and the second witness is that of our own spirit when we render service to God in that spirit of sonship—the disposition and attitude of mind that are consistent with the Holy Spirit's witness through his teaching on our sonship.

> *Verses 26-27: "Likewise the Spirit also helpeth our infirmities: for we know not how to pray as we ought: but the Spirit itself maketh intercession for us with groanings which cannot be uttered. And he that searcheth the hearts knoweth what is the mind of the spirit, because he maketh intercession for the saints according to the will of God."*

1. It should be observed, first of all, that if the Spirit of this passage means the Holy Spirit, its application would be to the

functioning of the Holy Spirit in heaven with God and Christ and the angels, and therefore would have no point in a discussion of "the personal Holy Spirit dwelling within us."

2. The context of the two verses indicates clearly that the groaning is done by the spirit of the one who is praying. The word groan is indicative of pain, either physical or mental, and there is no conceivable reason for the Holy Spirit to groan. Our own spirit groans with yearnings which we cannot utter, cannot vocalize or put in words, when we pray: "For we know not how to pray as we ought."

3. He who searches the heart and knows the mind of the Spirit is Christ, our intercessor—he knows the mind of the spirit of the one who is praying, but who cannot utter the yearnings of his heart. Christ our Intercessor knows the mind of our spirit and *He* intercedes for us. To make the Spirit here mean the Holy Spirit would have the Holy Spirit searching his own mind. And to make it mean that God knows the mind of the Holy Spirit could have no point—why all the talk about God knowing the mind of the Holy Spirit who is in heaven with him, when the Holy Spirit is an equivalent of the Spirit of God. It would amount to saying that God knows his own spirit.

4. The entire context is based on the initial statement: "For we know not how to pray as we ought." The infirmity mentioned has reference to the inability of the mind to put yearnings into words. But He who searches the heart knows the mind of the spirit the yearnings and the desires which it is unable to express—and in this way the spirit, our own spirit, helpeth our infirmity when He who searches the heart knows what is the mind of the spirit. There is but one divine Intercessor—Jesus Christ, not the Holy Spirit—and the "exegesis" of this verse, which has the personal Holy Spirit operating within us, has God, Christ, and the Holy Spirit mixed up and confused with the human spirit.

CAMPBELL'S COMMENTS

In Vol. I, beginning on page 111, of the *Millennial Harbinger*, under the caption, *Does The Holy Spirit Intercede For Christians,* Alexander Campbell wrote a lengthy treatise on Rom. 8:17-27, to prove that the context of this entire section referred to the groanings and intercessions of the human spirit and not of the Holy Spirit. A part of that treatise was recently reprinted in the *Firm Foundation.* Referring to the human spirit in Rom. 8:26, Campbell said:

> "I say, then, the (human) spirit itself speaks for us to God; it intercedes for our deliverance by groans which cannot be expressed in words. For although our spirit groans under these bodily afflictions and infirmities, and cannot give utterance to its own desires; yet when patiently bearing these trials, its groans have a meaning which is understood. Yes, he who searches the heart knows what these groans mean."

He further stated that he differed with all of his contemporaries who "made the spirit of man in verse 26, the Spirit of God; rather the spirit of patience, the Spirit of God in his official character." Again: "In the King's Translation it reads, 'He, or it, makes intercession for the saints according to the will of God.' Is it admissible to say that the Spirit of God, in this or any given case, makes intercession for the saints 'according' to the will of God, or according to God? The Spirit of God acting according to the will of God, in any case, implies an incongruity for which there is no analogy in the book of God." And he concludes with these words: "What a consolation to Christians that when groaning under afflictions, and unable how to express themselves, not knowing what to ask, their groans which they cannot turn into language have a meaning which God understands and regards."

THE WRITINGS OF THE REFORMERS
On these particular points of the eighth chapter of Romans, Lard surrenders by saying that "it is inexplicable"; and that "the mode of the dwelling we do not affect to understand"; and "to speak more definitely would not be wise to attempt." So Lard is a poor witness—his uncertain remarks contradict Campbell and are inconsistent with his own answer to J.B. Jeter in the *Review of Campbelism Examined.* As for Stone his uncertainties were many; at first he was confused with Presbyterian theology and turned to teaching in a Methodist academy; then he returned to the Presbyterians; later he joined in with the strange groups of the revivalists who were cataleptic, who swooned and had the jerks in his meetings; and he shifted many times before learning enough of the truth to separate himself from denominational parties. The immaturity of these men is evident in their own writings; they were young men emerging from the fog and confusion of Calvinism and all of the Confessions and Catechisms of medieval theology. The attempt to prove a position on the personal Holy Spirit indwelling by the changing views of these emerging men results in a sorry effort. Among these early men Campbell alone arrived at a mature and solid understanding of the full scope of the Holy Spirit's operations, influences, and effects upon and within the soul of man. When men appeal to such sources for support it serves only to reveal the insufficiency of their argument.

GALATIANS 4:6-7

> *"And because ye are sons, God hath sent forth the Spirit of his Son into your hearts, crying Abba, Father. Wherefore thou art no more a servant, but a son; and if a son, then an heir of God through Christ."*

The first seven verses of Galatians 4 connect with the last

verses of chapter 3, where the apostle had shown that the baptized Jews and Gentiles were together sons and heirs. The first seven verses of chapter 4 compare Judaism with the position of a minor who had not reached the status of sonship—an heir apparent who was yet a minor. But having been redeemed from the law they had "received the adoption of sons," and God had sent the spirit of sonship into their hearts, calling God Father.

SONS VERSUS SERVANTS

So the spirit of verse 6 is not the Holy Spirit, but the spirit of sonship, as the following verse specifies; "Wherefore thou art no more a servant, but a son; and if a son, then an heir of God through Christ." It is the same sonship and the same spirit of sons as in Rom. 8:15: "But ye have not received the spirit of bondage again to fear; but ye have received the spirit of adoption, whereby we cry Abba, Father." Here the spirit of adoption is in contrast with the spirit of bondage, and there is no reason for the small 's' on spirit of bondage and a large 'S' on spirit of adoption—for the spirit of adoption in Rom. 8: 15, and the spirit of sons in Gal. 4:6, do not refer to the Holy Spirit. There is no argument to be derived from these verses for the direct indwelling of the personal Holy Spirit.

One devotee of the direct personal Holy Spirit indwelling has said that these verses must refer to the Holy Spirit because only a person can cry. But David said, "so panteth my soul after thee, O God"—if the spirit can *pant,* it should be able to cry! Of course, the passage means that the spirit of the son calls God his Father. And the expression *Abba, Father* is only a combination of the Hebrew and Greek terms, and means Father, Father.

In Rom. 8:15 the apostle said that we receive the spirit of adoption, and in Gal. 4:6 he said that God *sent* the spirit of sonship into the heart. So the medium is of necessity the Word, for only by its teaching could we know anything of this adoption or of this sonship or of becoming "an heir of God through Christ."

OBJECTIONS TO DIRECT TESTIMONY

The objections to the theory of a direct testimony of the Holy Spirit to this sonship may be succinctly summed up:

1. The direct indwelling would set aside the fundamental principle that faith comes by hearing the Word of God, and would therefore become a miraculous knowledge proceeding from the direct witness of the Holy Spirit.

2. The direct witness of the Holy Spirit to sonship would reduce the number of witnesses to one instead of two. But the text of Rom. 8:15-17 states that the Spirit bears *witness with our spirit,* which means that the spirit of the son *responds* to the testimony of the Holy Spirit, and in the consistency of his attitude and disposition of sonship he thereby witnesses to the truth of the Spirit's testimony concerning the adoption of sons.

3. The direct witness of the Holy Spirit to sonship could be evinced only by the inner consciousness of feeling and is, therefore, based upon the same claims of evidence as *Spiritualism* for the communication of spirits; and of Catholics in the inner consciousness of the absolution of sins by the confessor; and of the heathen parent who immolates a child in belief that the gods are appeased by the offering; and of all the cults of the Holiness who lay claim to the direct witness and indwelling of the personal Holy spirit—the same facility with which one is established, all are established.

EPHESIANS 1:10-14

> *"That in the dispensation of the fullness of times he might gather together in one all things in Christ, both which are in heaven, and which are on earth; even in him: in whom also we have obtained an inheritance, being predestined according the purpose of him who worketh all things after the counsel of his own will. That we should be*

> *to the praise of his glory, who first trusted in Christ. In whom ye also trusted after that ye heard the word of truth, the gospel of your salvation: in whom also after that ye believed, ye were sealed with that Holy Spirit of promise, which is the earnest of our inheritance until the redemption of the purchased possession, unto the praise of his glory."*

Here again the function of the Holy Spirit is presented in the *dispensational* connection. All the parts of the former dispensation had been gathered together in one whole fulfillment in the new dispensation. The salvation of the Ephesian Gentiles by the Word of Truth was a part of that predestinated and fulfilled plan. It was the work of the Holy Spirit to reveal and seal and *guarantee* this divine plan. Through this revelation salvation came, in order "to the Jew first, and also to the Greek," as the apostle said to the Romans; and "that the Gentiles should be fellow heirs," as he said to the Ephesians." Following the order of this development Paul said: "we (apostles and Jews) should be to the praise of his glory, who first trusted in Christ"—the apostles were themselves the first in the order; then "in whom ye (the Gentiles) also trusted," after having heard the Word of Truth, which was the gospel that had saved them. In the acceptance of this Word of Truth they had been *sealed with that Holy Spirit of promise:* that is, the same promise that the Holy Spirit had given to the Jews on Pentecost, "for the promise is unto you and to your children (Jews), and to all that are afar off (Gentiles)—and it was that Holy Spirit of promise through the Word of Truth which was the seal and assurance to the Gentiles that in "the gospel of your salvation" they had entered into the same inheritance, the same possessed heritage of redemption as the Jews, signed, sealed, and stamped with the guarantee of the same Holy Spirit.

THE PERIOD OF CREATION
In harmony with the statement of verse 10, the whole argument of the apostle is dispensational. In the period of creation (Gen. 1) the Spirit brooded as a hovering bird to bring forth that which the Creator said, until the work of creation was finished. So in the period of the second creation the Holy Spirit brooded and hovered over the new church in the special gifts and powers and direction until it was finished in complete revelation. There was a direct sealing then, but the Word of Truth has been sealed. We have the seal and the stamp upon us, to be sure, but it is not the same in action—we have the *sign, seal,* and *brand* stamped on us through the Word of Truth.

THE SEAL OF THE SPIRIT
The meaning of a seal is a stamp, a brand, a guarantee, such as the seal of a state or a government on a document. It is a distinctive mark by which a thing can be known; it is something signed or branded by an instrument of authority, such as the letters of authority from the chief priests to persecute the church (Acts 9:2—26:10), and such as the Sanhedrin asked of Peter and John (Acts 4:7), "By what power (or authority) have ye done this?" The apostles had the stamp and the sign and the seal of the Holy Spirit on what they had preached and performed, that it was of God. This *stamp* of the Holy Spirit on us through the Word of Truth is the same seal but in different form or action—upon the apostles it was direct inspiration and power; upon us it is through the Word of Truth which bears the signature of the Holy Spirit as proof that it is of God. Every Christian today is sealed or stamped by the Holy Spirit as he follows its teaching.

The scriptural meaning and use of the word *seal* is made plain in the words of Christ in John 3:33-34. Referring to himself, Jesus said: "And what he hath seen and heard, that he testifieth; and no man receiveth his testimony. He that receiveth his testimony hath set to his seal that God is true. For he whom God hath sent speaketh the words of God: for God giveth not the Spirit by measure unto him." These verses refer to the testimony of God in and through Jesus Christ—"he that hath received his testimony hath set to his seal that God is true." It is plain that the word *seal* here denotes the *authority* which was stamped on the testimony that Christ had received from God. The statement "hath set to his seal that God is true" is followed by the explanation, "for he whom God hath sent speaketh the words of God: for God giveth not the Spirit by measure unto him." The Spirit which God had given to Christ without measure was the seal on the *words of God* that Christ had spoken. And it was the *authority* of the same Spirit that sealed "the word of truth" which the inspired apostle had preached to the Ephesians.

In this same sense of a stamped authority the same word *seal* is again used by Jesus in John 6:27: "Labor not for the meat which perisheth, but for that meat which endureth unto eternal life, which the Son of man shall give unto you: for him hath God the Father sealed." The meaning of the statement is unmistakable. God had sealed Jesus by the unlimited divine authority of his *spoken words,* by the Spirit without measure, which God had given to him. And that is how the Ephesians were sealed in Christ "with that Holy Spirit of promise" through the inspired *word of truth* which, the apostle assured the Ephesians, was "the gospel of your salvation." The theory of the direct indwelling of the personal Holy Spirit is not in the Ephesian passage—it is *not there.*

In 2 Cor. 1:21-22 it is stated that God had also sealed the apostles, and had given them the guarantee of the Spirit on their teaching: "Now he which establisheth us (apostles) with you (Corinthians) in Christ, and hath anointed us (apostles), is God; who hath also sealed us (apostles), and given us (apostles) the earnest of the Spirit in our (apostles) hearts." The same Spirit which Jesus said in John 3:33 had "set to his seal" that his spoken words were of God, had also sealed the teaching of the apostle Paul to the Corinthians and the Ephesians with the guarantee of inspiration. It was therefore in this same use of the word *seal*, in Eph. 1:13, that Paul assured the Ephesian Gentiles that the *seal of that Holy Spirit of promise* was to them the guarantee of their *equal heritage* with the Jews in the blessings of the gospel. There is no logical deduction from these passages in favor of the indwelling of the personal Holy Spirit in ordinary persons then or now. The consequential end of this theory of direct personal Holy Spirit possession would necessarily be inspiration and infallibility in the one who possessed the personal Holy Spirit. It is a theoretically false doctrine worthy only of rejection.

So *how* does the Holy Spirit seal us? By functioning through the apostles in the Word of Truth. The *We* and the *Ye* of this passage meant the *Apostles* and the *Ephesians.* In the miraculous period of the church it proceeded from the apostles to the church through inspiration; that period having been closed, the avenue through which it flows *now* is the Word of Truth, making no distinctions. The failure to make *dispensational* application of these Holy Spirit passages results in utter confusion and error.

THE EARNEST OF THE SPIRIT

The next question in the order is: What is the earnest of the Spirit? It has been repeatedly said that the earnest of this passage means the down payment of the direct indwelling of the personal Holy Spirit. In the first place, who said that the word in this text means a down payment? Paul did not say so nor teach so. Such an application is an example of stretching a figure of speech too far. Those who are making the word *earnest* mean a *down payment* are the users of the new translations—but the new versions take out the word *earnest* and put in such words as *assurance* and *pledge* and *guarantee*—so to hold on to their *down payment* they will fall back on the old version which they have all relegated!

But the word *earnest* in the old text is all right—it means *assurance,* and the assurance to the Gentiles of the same heritage of salvation with the Jews was the guarantee that had been stamped on the Word of Truth through the inspiration of the apostles. The new covenant was of God and had upon it the seal of the Holy Spirit. In this new covenant the Jews and the Gentiles together had the earnest of the Spirit—the assurance, pledge, and guarantee of their salvation. This seal and earnest of the Spirit is called *that Holy Spirit of promise,* and simply reverts to Pentecost: "For the promise is unto you, and to your children, and to all that are afar off, even as many as the Lord our God shall call." The Ephesian Gentiles were among them that were afar off in the heathen world and that Holy Spirit of promise was to them the seal and the assurance of their inheritance in the gospel of their salvation revealed to them through the Word of Truth. To call this assurance a down payment would place the Holy Spirit under debt; it beggars *that Holy Spirit of promise,* as though we cannot take his *word* for it; and it reveals how little regard these men have for the Word of Truth who are teaching this direct possession of the Holy Spirit doctrine. The facts of this passage do not sustain the doctrine of the direct personal Holy Spirit indwelling.

EPHESIANS 2:20-22

> *"And are built upon the foundation of the apostles and prophets, Jesus Christ himself being the chief corner stone; in whom all the building fitly framed together growth unto an holy temple in the Lord: in whom ye also are builded together for an habitation of God through the Spirit."*

It has been theorized that this passage means that God dwells in us representatively *in the Spirit,* and therefore, though the indwelling of God is representative, the indwelling of the Spirit is personal. The preposition in the phrase *through the Spirit* is *en,* and according to the authorities it stands for *by* or *with* or *in* or *through,* and there are passages having all of these prepositions derived from the *en* connected with the Spirit of this passage—so the text itself determines its use.

THE HABITATION OF GOD

It is clear that verses 20 and 21 describe the building together of the Jews and the Gentiles into the church—they were *fitly framed together* and *builded together* into the church, for the habitation of God. This framing and building together of the Jews and the Gentiles was through or by the agency and work of the Holy Spirit—the Spirit built the church with the material of Jews and Gentiles for God's habitation—it is the church, not the individual, in this passage that is the habitation of God, and the Holy Spirit was the divine agency of its construction. That is, it was in or *through* or *by* the teaching of the Spirit that the Jews and Gentiles were builded together into the church for God's habitation. In verse 21 the apostle compares the church to a temple, which among the Gentiles was the habitation for their gods. But the church is *the temple of the living God,* and it is built through (by) the Spirit for God's habitation.

CONSTRUCTED BY THE SPIRIT

In verses 16-18 of this chapter the apostle mentions that the Jews and the Gentiles were reconciled unto God in the one body *by the Spirit.* In verse 19 it is called the household of God; and in verses 20-22 the functioning of the Holy Spirit in the building of the church with the material of the Jews and the Gentiles is described. In chapter 3:6 it mentions that the Jews and the Gentiles are fellow-heirs in *the same body;* and chapter 4:4 affirms that there is only *one body* and describes its components. The entire context represents the church as the building which was constructed through or by the Spirit for the habitation of God. And *how* did the Holy Spirit build the Jews and the Gentiles together into this structure? The apostle answers that question in 1 Cor. 12:13: "For by one Spirit (the teaching of the Spirit) we are all baptized into one body (the church), whether we be Jews or Gentiles, whether we be bond or free; and have been all made to drink into one Spirit." To drink into *the one Spirit,* of course, means to imbibe the teaching of the Spirit. And it is by and through the teaching of the Spirit that we are builded together in the church, which is the habitation of God. These verses do not teach that the personal Holy Spirit inhabits a person, and they afford no proof for the direct indwelling doctrine.

EPHESIANS 3:16

> *"That he would grant you according to the riches of his glory, to be strengthened with might by his Spirit in the inner man."*

The phrase *by his Spirit* here expresses the agency of the Spirit: In 1 Cor. 12:3 the apostles said that "no man can say that Jesus is Lord, but by the Holy Spirit"—which certainly does not mean that the Holy Spirit is in every man that says Jesus is Lord; it is only by the teaching of the Holy Spirit that anyone could know and therefore say that Jesus is Lord. So it is by the teaching of the Spirit that the inner man is strengthened.

THE SPIRIT THROUGH KNOWLEDGE

And here is a parallel and an equation: Col. 1:10-11—"increasing in the knowledge of God, strengthened with all might, according to his glorious power"; and Eph. 3:16, "Strengthened with might by his Spirit in the inner man." The Colossian passage states that we are *strengthened with might* in the knowledge of God; and the Ephesian passage states that we are *strengthened with might* in the Spirit of God. The knowledge of God does not refer to what God knows—it means what God has revealed by the Holy Spirit for us to know—it is the Word of the Spirit. Therefore when a Christian is strengthened in the knowledge of the Word, he is by that means and medium strengthened in the Spirit—and when the *knowledge* that the Spirit has revealed is in the inner man, the *Spirit* is in the inner man through that knowledge. The attempt to make this text mean the direct indwelling of the Holy Spirit *apart from the word* is not only irresponsible, it is downright arbitrary.

BY THE SPIRIT THROUGH THE TRUTH

For another analogy, compare 1 Pet. 1:22 with Eph. 3:16. The apostle Peter said: "Seeing that ye have purified your souls in obeying the truth through (by) the Spirit." The preposition in the phrase *through the Spirit* in this verse is *dia,* and the preposition in the phrase *by the Spirit* in Eph. 3:16, is *dia,* and the passages are prepositionally parallel—so if *through* or *by* the Spirit in 1 Pet. 1:22 does not mean a direct operation on the souls of sinners then *through* or *by* the Spirit in Eph. 3:16 does not mean a direct indwelling in the inner man of Christians.

The apostle Paul said to these Ephesians elders in Acts 20:32: "I commend you to God, and to the word of his grace, which is able to build you up, and to give you an inheritance among them that are sanctified." The effort now being made to prove that the Word of God is insufficient and inadequate proves rather that we have men among us who are far-out in their doctrine of the Holy Spirit.

EPHESIANS 5:18-19

> *"And be not drunk with wine, wherein is excess;*
> *but be filled with the Spirit; speaking to yourselves*
> *in psalms and hymns and spiritual songs, singing*
> *and making melody in your heart to the Lord."*

The phrase *"be filled with the Spirit"* is the imperative mood, and carries a command—it is a command to obey, a thing in which the one subject to it is active. The command of Col. 3:16 is its parallel: "Let the word of Christ dwell in you richly in all wisdom; teaching and admonishing one another in psalms and hymns and spiritual songs, singing with grace in your hearts to the Lord." The same apostle was writing on the same subject to the respective churches and the phrases in both passages are in the imperative mood and carry parallel commands: *Be filled with the Spirit—Let the word of Christ dwell in you richly.* This is an equation—Eph. 5:18 is equated with Col. 3:16. In Eph. 5:18 we are *commanded* to be filled with the Spirit, and in Colossians 3:16 we are told how to obey the command.

THE PARALLEL OF EPH. 5:18 AND COL. 3:16

But we have been told in quite a scholarly fashion that the two passages are not "completely parallel," and that the argument is not "sound reasoning" because in Luke 1:41 Elisabeth "was filled with the Holy Spirit" when "the babe leaped in her womb." Now, that is a queer comment to come from a pedantic professor. First, two things are either parallel or they are not; a *parallel* is *complete* or it is not parallel; the remark that the references are not completely parallel implies that two things may be incompletely parallel. Second, the illustration of Elisabeth does not illustrate, for the reason that when she *was filled with the Spirit* she was not obeying any command but was being acted upon. There is quite a difference in the phrases *be filled with the Spirit* and *was filled with the Spirit.* To the Ephesians the command *be filled* is the active imperative, a thing in the doing of which the person acts; but in the case of Elisabeth, *was filled* is passive, and she was acted upon.

Take the examples of Zacharias and Mary in the same chapter, along with Elisabeth: when Zacharias *was filled* with the Spirit, he *prophesied;* when Elisabeth *was filled* with the Spirit, the babe leaped in her womb, and she *prophesied;* and the angel told Mary, who had not known man, that "the Holy Spirit *shall come upon* thee." In these instances there were no commands to be obeyed, Zacharias, Elisabeth, and Mary were passive, they were acted upon; what occurred was done for them. But in Eph. 5:18 *be filled with the Spirit* was a command to be obeyed, something to be done by the subjects addressed, and, as applied to us, it is something *we do.*

WHAT *BE FILLED* MEANS

The immediate receptions of the Holy Spirit were not commands to obey; the Holy Spirit baptism was not a command to obey; the spiritual gifts were not commands to obey; and the direct indwelling of the personal Holy Spirit could not be obeyed—but *be filled with the Spirit* in Eph. 5:18 was Paul's *command* to the Ephesians for them to obey—and *let the word of Christ dwell in you richly* in Col. 3:16 was Paul's definition of *how* the command is obeyed. These were instructions on precisely the same subject to the respective churches. They are parallel—the two passages are equated—and the command to "let the word of Christ dwell in you richly" is equal to the command "be filled with the Spirit."

We fill the field with *wheat* by sowing it with the seed. We fill the garden with flowers by planting in it the seeds. We fill the physical self with food by *eating.* We fill the heart with the Spirit when we sow our soul's inner world with the spiritual seed of the Word. The command *to be filled with the Spirit* means: Fill up your hearts with the rich Word of God. Jeremiah said: "Thy words were found, and I did eat them."

EPHESIANS 6:10

> *"And take the helmet of salvation, and the sword of the Spirit, which is the word of God."*

It is said that the Word is the sword that the Holy Spirit uses. Rather, the Word of God is the sword that the Holy Spirit forged for us to use. The Spirit does not wield the sword—we ourselves wield it, and if we do not wield it, then it will not be wielded. If the Holy Spirit performs some direct operation in wielding the sword, the action and the method should be subject to definition and description, and demonstration. When the direct powers of the Spirit were being exercised there existed also the demonstrations to prove them. *As goes the proposition, so must be the demonstration:* If the Holy Spirit operates apart from, without, and in addition to the Word, then why forge the sword at all?

The old time-worn theology of the insufficiency of the Word of God is the root of the whole movement now in motion within the brotherhood. But the Word is sufficient: it is "quick and powerful"—living and active—"and sharper than any two-edged sword." As the smith forges instruments and weapons, the Holy Spirit by inspiration in the apostles of Christ forged the sword of the Word for us to wield: "And the things that thou hast heard of me... the same commit thou to faithful men, who shall be able to teach others also," said Paul to Timothy (2 Tim. 2:2), and that is how the Spirit works now.

1 THESSALONIANS 1:5

"For our gospel came not unto you in word only, but also in power, and in the Holy Spirit, and in much assurance; as ye know what manner of men we were among you for your sake."

The apostolic statement that "our gospel came not unto you in word only" referred to the incident of Paul's first preaching in Thessalonica. The verb *came* is past tense. The passage does not say that the gospel *comes* not unto you in word only—it *came* not unto the Thessalonians in word only. The expression "our gospel" meant the gospel Paul first preached to the Thessalonians; and "in power and in the Holy Spirit" meant that his preaching was accompanied by signs and miracles as a demonstration of "what manner of men we were among you"—that is, men possessing extraordinary powers of inspiration. But at that time the

Thessalonians were aliens; it was before their conversion. So the use of this passage to prove a direct reception of the Spirit now would also prove a direct operation of the Spirit in the conversion of alien sinners. Will the claimants of the direct indwelling accept *that exegesis?* Anything that proves too much proves nothing.

The evident meaning of the passage is that when Paul first preached the gospel to the Thessalonians, it was not in word only because it was attended by the power of the Holy Spirit wrought in signs and miracles to prove what manner of men—that is, men with the extraordinary powers of inspiration. The Thessalonian passage compares with the same apostle's statement to the Romans—chapter 15:19—concerning the things God had wrought by him "through mighty signs and wonders, by the power of the Spirit of God," to demonstrate their word, and thus "make the Gentiles obedient" to the gospel.

The charge of Paul to Timothy is again urgent: "Study to show thyself approved unto God, a workman that needeth not to be ashamed, rightly dividing the word of truth." This lack of knowing the proper division of the Word is more than surprising, it is amazing.

1 PETER 1:12

> *"Unto whom it was revealed, that not unto themselves, but unto us they did minister the things, which are now reported unto you by them that have preached the gospel unto you with the Holy Spirit sent down from heaven."*

As surprising as it may seem the phrase "with the Holy Spirit sent down from heaven" has been recently employed to teach that the Holy Spirit performs direct operations today in addition to the Word. A cursory look at the text will show the connection of verse 12 with verses 10 and 11 concerning the salvation that had been prophesied—foretold by the prophets—and that the apostles reported the fulfillment of these prophecies when they preached this salvation by the inspiration of the Holy Spirit. The phrase *with the Holy Spirit sent down from heaven* refers to the miraculous demonstrations, mentioned in Rom. 15:19, by which the preaching of the apostles was confirmed "through mighty signs and wonders, by the power of the Spirit of God" that accompanied their ministry. If the Holy Spirit were *sent down from heaven* now, there would of necessity be the presence of *signs,* for as goes the proposition so must be the demonstration. Where is the proof?

The claim of *personal experience* is not evidence—the one who offers *personal testimony* merely attempts to prove something by *himself* and the proof needed is the sign to demonstrate the claim. If the Holy Spirit is *sent* today as it was in the 1 Pet. 1:12 passage, the one upon whom it is sent does not differ from and is not inferior to the apostles of Christ—and with such *inspired men* among us there would be no need for the *revealed* and *written* Word.

1 JOHN 2:20, 27

> *"But ye have an unction from the Holy One, and ye know all things... But the anointing which ye have received of him abideth in you, and ye need not that any should teach you: but as the same anointing teacheth you all things, and is truth, and is no lie, and even as it hath taught you, ye shall abide in him."*

The reference to the Holy One here is the basis for the claim that "the anointing which ye have received of him abideth in you," mentioned in verse 27, is the indwelling of the Spirit which is not produced by the Word. The anointing of this passage in other renditions is called an "unction," and has evident reference to the spiritual gifts that still remained in the church when the first epistle of John was written. In the same verse it states the result of this unction or anointing: "And ye need not that any man teach you: but as the same anointing teacheth you of all things, and is truth." This unction is described as an impartation, a special endowment belonging to the Spiritual Gifts era, so that those possessing it needed not to be taught—that is, on the particular things that pertained to the unction. It appears to have bearing on discerning false teaching and judging the deceivers, and as thus guided they could reject the deceivers who were described as *antichrist*. This anointing did not continue, but passed out with all other spiritual gifts of the apostolic age. It appears altogether infeasible to apply this passage to the indwelling of the Spirit now, in the light of the statement that the one possessing it had no need of teaching, but was taught by the anointing. During the apostolic age the specially endowed teachers were necessary to the teaching and edification of the church, but these indwellings did not continue, and to apply this and other passages to a personal indwelling of the Holy Spirit in the Christian today is a complete misfire. MacKnight's commentary renders this passage in this paraphrase: "Although I know that the gift of discerning spirits, which you have received from the Holy Spirit, remaineth in you and that you have no need that any one should teach you how to judge of these deceivers and their doctrines, unless to exhort you to judge of them, as the same gift teacheth you concerning all things... wherefore, as it hath taught you that these teachers are antichrists, reject their doctrine, and abide in the truth concerning him." That is the exact meaning of 1 John 2:27, and it has no reference to the influence of the Holy Spirit upon or in us.

1 JOHN 3:24

> *"And he that keepeth his commandments dwelleth in him, and he in him. And hereby we know that he abideth in us, by the Spirit which he*

hath given us."

The *abiding* of the Spirit here is equated with *keeping* the commandments, just as the *indwelling Spirit* in Eph. 5:16 is equated with the *indwelling word* in Col. 3:16. The apostle's teaching here is extended into the next verses of 1 John 4:1-6 and is concluded with the statement: "We are of God: he that knoweth God heareth us; he that is not of God, heareth not us. Hereby know we the spirit of truth, and the spirit of error." The Spirit which God has given to us is here plainly defined as the spirit of truth in the apostles of Christ. It is by hearing the teaching that the Spirit abides in us.

The Holy Spirit crusaders want to equate the Holy Spirit with personal experiences and direct impressions, as all of the "Holy Ghost cults" have always done. But in these verses the apostle John equates the Holy Spirit with the spirit of truth, and the abiding of the Spirit with the hearing of the truth. "Hereby we know," he said. Shall we accept the religion of *knowledge,* or shall we resort to a religion of *feelings* and join the Holy Rollers!

1 JOHN 5:9-10.

> *"If we receive the witness of men, the witness of God is greater: for this is the witness of God which he hath testified of his Son. He that believeth on the Son of God hath the witness in himself."*

It is here asserted that the statement "hath witness in himself" establishes the immediate indwelling of the Holy Spirit, resulting in personal experience. In the context of these verses there are three important words: *witness, testify* and *record*—and these three words represent the one Greek term in the forms *martureo* and *marturea,* meaning to bear record, to witness, and to testify. The witness which one has in himself is defined in verse 9: "For this is the witness of God which he hath testified of his Son." So the witness that is greater than men, which one has in himself, is the testimony of the Holy Spirit through the truth, "because the Spirit is truth"—verse 6. The reason the witness one has in *himself* is greater than men is here stated: *because the Spirit is truth.* There can be no greater witness than the Holy Spirit's truth. The Holy Spirit beareth witness with our spirit through the truth, through the written word embraced in the heart.

THE CAMPBELL CONCLUSION

It is appropriate here once more to quote the words of Alexander Campbell: He affirmed that "all arguments and persuasions of the Holy Spirit are found in the written word"; and stated that it is an assumption to claim "that the Spirit operates *sometimes* without the word"; and concluded, "therefore *only* must mean *always* through the word." Otherwise, Campbell continued, the theory would have "the naked spirit of God operating on the naked spirit of man, without argument or motive, interposed in some direct, mysterious, inexplicable way to incubate the soul and make it spiritually alive, by direct immediate contact, without intervention of moral or spiritual ideas communicated through truth." His clever antagonist, N.L. Rice, could not with all of his satire overcome this basic principle, and the direct indwelling advocates among us now will not find themselves able to do so.

CONSEQUENCES OF DIRECT INDWELLING

There are some basic doctrinal consequences attached to the current explosive Holy Spirit revolution that should be seriously considered:

First, it is the revival of the old theology which has been repeatedly refuted in earlier years—the dogma of "the sinful nature of man" and the necessity of the direct impact of the Spirit to remove it, with the subsequent effect of the impossibility of apostasy through the indwelling presence of the Holy Spirit. Lately, we have been hearing the phrase "our sinful nature" in the parlance of some of our preachers. But man does not inherit a *sinful nature*—the spirit comes from God, and that language is the shibboleth of the sectarian dogma of original sin.

Second, it is contrary to the nature of man, in that all direct operations and indwellings circumvent the faculties of man to which the revelation of the Holy Spirit is addressed.

Third, it is contrary to the nature of God's Law, which is designated the law *of the mind* because it pertains to the mind and is addressed to the mind, and therefore named the law *of the mind.*

Fourth, it contradicts the teaching of the New Testament on both the law of pardon and means of edification.

Fifth, if the personal Holy Spirit dwells within anyone, his conduct is guided by direct Holy Spirit control, apart from the word; and if that is true of his conduct it would also be true of his words, and the result would be inspiration.

Sixth, the direct operation and indwelling propaganda surrenders the whole gospel scheme of things and all argument against the doctrine of the denominations collapses. These are a few of the many erroneous consequences of the current Holy Spirit revolution. The failure of the whole movement is the lack of discrimination between the special endowments of the provisional miraculous period and the general influence and work of the Holy Spirit through divine revelation in the permanent form and order.

Seventh, in consequence of the theory of the direct Holy Spirit operation and indwelling, Paul's reference to "the natural man" in 1 Cor. 2:14 has been characteristically misapplied: "But the natural man receiveth not the things of the Spirit of God: for they are foolishness unto him: neither can he know them, because they are spiritually discerned." The new versions change the words of this important passage. The RSV rewrites the verse to make it teach the theological dogma that the unregenerate, unspiritual person *cannot understand* the teaching of the Spirit; and the NEB makes it read *cannot grasp* the teaching of the Spirit. But Paul did not say that the unregenerate *cannot understand* and *cannot grasp—he* said *the natural man receiveth not the things of the Spirit.* There is a vast difference in the phrases *cannot understand* and *receiveth not.* The natural man is the man of natural knowledge mentioned by the apostle in the preceding first chapter of Corinthians, in contrasting human philosophy with divine revelation. The man of natural knowledge cannot receive the things of *revelation* through his human channels of information or knowledge. The chemist, the geologist, the astronomer, and all scientists are classifications of the natural man. The chemist cannot receive the things of revelation through the chemical experiments of his laboratory; the geologist cannot receive the knowledge that is within the sphere of revelation through his drill; the astronomer, peering through his telescope into the heavens, may ascertain things astronomical and astrophysical, but he cannot receive through his telescope the knowledge that belongs to the revealed things of the Spirit. The natural man is the man of natural knowledge which Paul declared could not receive nor ascertain through his natural means of knowledge the things within the sphere of revelation and inspiration.

The denominational debaters in past years used this Corinthian passage as an argument for the direct operation of the Holy Spirit on the *unspiritual* or *unregenerated* man, to remove his *sinful nature,* so that by regeneration he could *understand* the spiritual things. All of the older gospel preachers and debaters refuted such arguments—and now we hear some of our preachers of today quoting the new versions to make 1 Cor. 2:14 mean that the *unsaved* man cannot *understand* the things of the Spirit! It is the unmitigated false doctrine of the theological dogmas of original sin, the direct operation of the Holy Spirit, and the impossibility of apostasy—the theological triplets of orthodox denominational creeds, the theories of which we have exposed and refuted through all the years of the existence of the church on this continent. Shall we now yield the ground gained by contesting every inch of it in the defense of the truth against all such error, and which we have continued to occupy by the preaching of the gospel by the mighty phalanx of gospel preachers in the past? These consequences may be denied, but they exist as the logical conclusions from the direct operation and personal indwelling of the Holy Spirit.

The apostle's conclusion in the last two verses of the chapter is evidence that he was contrasting the realm of natural knowledge with the sphere of divine revelation: "But he that is spiritual judgeth all things, yet he himself is judged of no man. For who hath known the mind of the Lord that he should instruct him? But we have the mind of Christ." The spirit-inspired man judged all *revealed things* by the inspiration that was in him—and the apostle's conclusion was: "We have the mind of Christ"; that is, the inspired apostles had *the knowledge of Christ* received through the channel of *revelation* and *inspiration* and not through the sources of human knowledge by the natural man.

To me it is a strange thing that these truths are not known and understood by professors and preachers today, and it is my own considered opinion that the source of it is the theologies of the Seminaries from which our professors have obtained their *Divinity Degrees,* together with the effect of the impact of the modernisms of the Neo-Orthodox Movement on the schools, the professors, the preachers and the churches of our present generation. May God preserve the Bible and save the church.

Chapter Six:
The Baptism of the Holy Spirit

The commencement of the mission of the Holy Spirit in the world was simultaneous with the initiation of the scheme of redemption and the inauguration of the kingdom of heaven. In the centuries and the millenniums of time this divine plan of redemption was hidden in the omniscient mind of God, unknown to angels or men. When the time came in the wisdom of God for the gracious system of salvation to be revealed, He assigned that function to the Holy Spirit. The antecedent premises for its accomplishment were the advent and ministry of the Christ, and the preparation for the establishment of the kingdom foretold by the prophets and announced by John and Jesus. In Mark 9:1, the Lord said to the disciples: "There be some of them that stand here, which shall not taste of death, till they have seen the kingdom of God come with power." And in Acts 1:8, to the disciples in Jerusalem, he said: "Ye shall receive power, after that the Holy Spirit is come upon you." And in Acts 2:1-4 the descent of the Holy Spirit is described. Thus from the banks of the Jordan where Jesus was baptized, to the hill of Calvary where he was crucified, his teaching pointed to Pentecost.

POINTING TO PENTECOST

Every function assigned to and every operation or influence performed or exerted by the Holy Spirit upon or within men are all connected with the Holy Spirit's dispensation, beginning on Pentecost. The announcement of John the Baptist, the promise of Christ to the apostles, and the Lord's teaching concerning the presence, power, and performance of the Holy Spirit were all Pentecost pointers.

First of all in this consideration was the announcement of the

Forerunner in Luke 3:16-17: "I indeed baptize you with water; but one mightier than I cometh, the latchet of whose shoes I am not worthy to unloose: he shall baptize you with the Holy Spirit and with fire." The announcement here made was that there would be the Holy Spirit baptism, but it assuredly did not mean that the promise of it was to all who were in John's audience—hence, in the clause, "he shall baptize you," the pronoun *you* was not intended as a general promise but merely an announcement of something that would occur. It has been claimed that the use of the pronoun *you* in the plural means that the Holy Spirit baptism was promised to the whole audience of hearers. Some comparisons of the use of the plural you in other instances, particularly in the apostolic epistles, will show that even though an epistle was addressed to whole churches, in certain parts of it the pronoun *you* was applicable to only certain ones among them. The Corinthian epistles were addressed to the entire church, yet in numerous passages the pronoun *you* applied to only some of them, as clearly indicated, as an example, in chapters 4:8, 14, 21 and 6:7, 8, 11, the last verse of which citations makes the application of the *you* to the *some* to which it applied. Other examples are abundant. That John's announcement of the Holy Spirit applied only to the apostles, and pointed to Pentecost, is settled by the Lord himself in Acts 1:4-5: "And, being assembled together with them, commanded them that they should not depart from Jerusalem, but wait for the promise of the Father, which saith he, ye have heard of me. For John truly baptized with water; but ye shall be baptized with the Holy Spirit not many days hence." These words of Christ prove solidly that the Holy Spirit baptism was a promise to the apostles, and that it was fulfilled on the *Day of Pentecost* in Acts 2:1-4. It is evident, therefore, that the Spirit baptism was a promise to the apostles alone, and pointed to Pentecost, and to the Holy Spirit's dispensation; so that all who accepted the teaching of the apostles obtained the benefits of the

Holy Spirit baptism received by the apostles. It was special in promise, but general in effect.

THE WHEAT AND THE CHAFF

In connection with the Holy Spirit baptism announcement of John, it should not be overlooked that the promise was twofold: "He shall baptize you with the Holy Spirit and with fire." The question here is: What was the baptism with fire, and who were to be its subjects? The following verse—Luke 3:17—gives the answer to that question "Whose fan is in his hand, and he will thoroughly purge his floor, and will gather the wheat into the garner; but the chaff he will burn with fire unquenchable." The use of the word *fan* here referred to the ancient process of separating the wheat from the chaff. The part of the nation of Israel that accepted Christ is here classified as the *wheat,* but that part of the Jewish nation that rejected Christ is designated the *chaff.* The gathering of the wheat into the garner meant the entrance of the Jews who accepted Christ into the new institution and the benefits of the Holy Spirit's dispensation; and the burning of the chaff with *fire unquenchable* meant the total destruction of the nation of Israel.

This was the axe that was laid at the root of the tree of fleshly Israelism, mentioned in verses 7 to 9, which were preliminary to John's announcement of the Spirit and fire baptism, the application of which is plainly put in these withering words: "Then said he to the multitude that came forth to be baptized of him, O generation of vipers, who hath warned you to flee from the wrath to come? Bring forth therefore fruits worthy of repentance, and begin not to say within yourselves, We have Abraham to our fathers: for I say unto you, That God is able of these stones to raise up children unto Abraham. And now also the axe is laid at the root of the trees: every tree therefore which bringeth not forth fruit is hewn down, and cast into the fire." The axe was laid at the root of the tree of Israelism—it was cut down *root and branch* with nothing left to sprout again. And the phrase *cast into the fire* explains the meaning of fire in verse 17—the total destruction and end of the rejecting nation of Israel.

THE FUNCTION OF THE COMFORTER

Second in the order of announcements of the Holy Spirit's dispensation was the Lord's promise to his apostles of the *Comforter,* which he would send after his departure from them and his return to the Father. This *Comforter* was the *Paracletos* for which term there is no English correspondent. It might have been anglicized, or "english-ized," to read *Paraclete,* which still would be the promise of something to the apostles alone which would fill the place of Jesus with them. Because Jesus said, in the text of John 14:16-26, "I will not leave you comfortless," the noun *Comforter* was applied to this promise as the name for it. But we are not left to surmise what it designates: "I will pray the Father, and he shall give you another Comforter... even the Spirit of truth: whom the world cannot receive." The *Comforter* therefore was the measure of the Holy Spirit possessed by the apostles for the revelation of the truth—"the Spirit of truth," or complete inspiration, and was promised only to the apostles of Christ.

The phrase "whom the world cannot receive" does not refer to the alien sinner not receiving a direct operation of the Holy Spirit. There are numerous passages by which to disprove that contention, without using a passage that does not refer to it. The term *world* here has reference to men in general as opposite to the *apostles* of Christ, and it means that this promise was *special* and not *general;* it was a promise to the apostles alone, and to no one else. The proof of this affirmation is seen in the functions ascribed to the *Comforter* in chapters 14:26, and 16:13. The *Comforter* would "bring all things to your remembrance whatsoever I have said unto you" and "he will guide you into all truth." Here is stated the two-fold office of the Holy Spirit Comforter in the apostles: first, the *reminding office* of the Holy Spirit in them:

"bring all things to your remembrance"; and second, the *revealing office* of the Holy Spirit in them—"he shall teach you all things" and "he will guide you into all truth." The Lord did not teach his apostles "all things" or "all truth" while he was with them—this he said in chapter 16:16: "I have yet many things to say unto you, but ye cannot bear them now" but when "the Spirit of truth is come, he will guide you into all truth." It was therefore reserved for the *Comforter,* the Holy Spirit of inspiration, to reveal to the apostles the things that the Lord had not Himself told them, and thus complete the gospel plan of redemption. It is apparent, therefore, that the promise of the *Comforter* was made to the apostles alone.

The men chosen to be his apostles were to be forever the teachers of the world—not for their time only, but for all time—and it was imperative that there should be no mistake in recalling the words of Christ, and no error in their teaching. For that reason they were told that the *Comforter* would "bring all things to your remembrance whatsoever I have said unto you," so their recollection might be faultless; and "he shall teach you all things" and "he will guide you into all truth," so their teaching might be without error. It is evident that these words were addressed to the apostles alone, and that the promise of the *Comforter* was not a general promise, but a special promise to the apostles.

But this function of the *Paraclete* required a means, and that means or medium was the truth—"even the Spirit of truth"—and that was inspiration, the inspired Word, the Word of Truth. The further saying "that he may abide with you forever" and "shall be in you" enhanced the promise that through the apostles the *Paraclete* would be mankind's teacher forever—and that teaching is as *apostolic* today as when the *inspiration* was communicated in the words of their tongues and pens. To make a general application of this special promise cancels the mission of the *Paraclete* to the apostles.

It is claimed that the words of Jesus to the apostles that the *Comforter* would be *with* them and *in* them proves that it is not *impossible* for the Holy Spirit to dwell within a person. If that is true, it would only prove that such an indwelling would be miraculous, and would therefore be *impossible without miraculous process and intervention.* And as the miraculous order ended with inspiration, there could be no such action upon or entrance into any person today of the personal Holy Spirit. But Jesus did not say that the personal *Holy Spirit* would be in the apostles—he said "even the Spirit of truth"—it was *the Spirit* in them through *inspiration.* The Lord s statement in John 14:17 that "the Spirit of truth... dwelleth with you, and shall be in you" referred to the power of the Holy Spirit in the apostles, as stated in Luke 24:49 and Acts 1:8—"endued with power from on high" and "ye shall receive power, after that the Holy Spirit is come upon you." It seems that anyone who is not looking the other way could see that John 14:17 refers to the power and *inspiration* of the Holy Spirit in the apostles, and not the personal Holy Spirit dwelling within a person. No such conclusion can be derived from the premises of these passages—nor *from any other passage.*

There is another consequence involved in that fallacy: If it is true that the promise of Christ to the apostles that the Holy Spirit would be *in* them proves that it is *possible* for the personal Holy Spirit to dwell in a person now, it would also prove that all of the *powers* resulting from such Holy Spirit inhabitation would be possible today. May as well claim that the power of tongues in the apostles which enabled them to speak every language without having learned them proves that it is possible to employ the power of tongue-speaking today, and all of the other powers belonging to a direct personal Holy Spirit possession. The existence of such a thing would require the repetition of the miraculous occurrences of Pentecost, and a continuation of the miraculous dispensation which ended with the apostolic age.

The current agitation on tongue-speaking evidently stems from this theory of the direct personal Holy Spirit indwelling. It is the generator of this incipient movement within the churches in some quarters and is giving it momentum, the promoters of which are attempting to be consistent with the direct-indwelling theory; whereas the professors who teach the personal Holy Spirit indwelling, but reject the exercise of its powers, are inconsistent in holding to the theory but denying its consequences.

THE CLOTHING WITH POWER

It must be further postulated that this Comforter was synonymous with the baptism of the Holy Spirit, which also was a promise to the apostles only. Properly defined, the Holy Spirit baptism was *the clothing with power* which came to the apostles on Pentecost. in the promise of Luke 24:49 the Lord said they should be "endued with power from on high," otherwise translated, "clothed with power"; and in Acts 2:4 on the day of Pentecost the waiting apostles "were all filled with the Holy Spirit." It was not the manner of the Holy Spirit's descent from heaven that constituted the baptism of the Spirit, but their being *filled* or *overwhelmed,* or *endued* and *clothed*—it was the result, not the manner of descent, that defines the Holy Spirit baptism, which the apostles only received. If any power of the Holy Spirit was lacking, it could not have been the *overwhelming,* or the baptism, and it is therefore a mistake to assume that others than the apostles, who received certain measures or were subjects of certain manifestations of the Spirit were thereby recipients of the Holy Spirit baptism.

It is sometimes insisted that 1 Corinthians 12:13, "For by one spirit are we all baptized into one body," makes the baptism of the Holy Spirit general. But the preposition *by* expresses the agency, not the element of the baptism of this verse. The agent of baptism cannot also be the element, and the Spirit, through the teaching of the Spirit, was the agent of the baptism. The passage is this: By one Spirit (the teaching) are we all baptized (immersed in water) into one body (the church)... and have all been made to drink into (participate in the blessings of) one Spirit." There is no Holy Spirit baptism in this or any other passage referring to others than the apostles of Christ.

As an example of how far this erroneous teaching on the Holy Spirit has been extended, in the R.B. Sweet Company's current literature series there is a "teenage" booklet which purports to advise *teenagers* how to make the *Comforter* their counsellor, thus applying to the young people in the church that measure and function of the Holy Spirit which was promised only to the apostles of Christ for the purpose of inspiration. And it was this same series that recently had a primary lesson teaching the children to *pray for the Holy Spirit.* This company is evidently using the Sunday School literature of denominational publishing companies (as some others among us are doing) and their editors do not know how to sift out the erroneous denominational doctrine which saturates their literature. And the children and young people of some of our churches are being made the victims of this sort of thing.

It is this same company that is forcing the use of that *official version* of the Neo-Orthodox National Council of Churches—the new so-called *Revised Standard Version*—on the churches through their literature series, and they have announced a *new commentary* based on that perversion of the Bible. All of the dependable concordances and dictionaries, and reliable versions, have been based on the texts that produced the book that has been the Bible of the centuries, and is still the Bible. These late versions have gone wild. Their translators are perverters, and like designing men, their subtle language exposes their character and reveals their *purpose—the destruction of the Bible.*

The elders of the churches need to know these sources of wrong teaching. What people do privately is their personal business, but what is done and taught in the churches is the responsibility of the elders—and God will not hold them guiltless who allow such false teaching to invade the congregations. The same thing applies to the teaching of the Bible in the colleges—what is taught in the Bible departments is the responsibility of the trustees and administration of the school. There is no such thing as academic *freedom* to teach religious error in Bible departments of the schools—the *Bible is the Word of God.*

After the death of Alexander Campbell his Bethany College passed into the control of the modernist group of the Christian Church and is today a hotbed of modernism. There are some definite signs that our brotherhood has some *Bethanys* developing in our midst.

THE CASE OF CORNELIUS

The bearing of the conversion of Cornelius on the subject of the Holy Spirit baptism has been much discussed, with the generally prevailing idea that Cornelius was the recipient of Holy Spirit baptism. A study of what Holy Spirit baptism was, the purpose of it and the power it imparted, will substantiate, I believe, my own conviction that the manifestation of the Holy Spirit at the house of Cornelius, as recorded in the tenth and eleventh chapters of Acts, was not Holy Spirit baptism. The statement of Peter, "Then remembered I the word of the Lord, how that he said, John indeed baptized with water; but ye shall be baptized with the Holy Spirit,"—("not many days hence," Acts 1:5)—indicates only that this occurrence reminded Peter of what had occurred on Pentecost; and he continued to say, "Forasmuch as God gave unto them (the Gentiles) the like gift as he did unto us (apostles)"—it was a *like gift,* not the same thing, and was like it only in the manner in which it had descended upon them as a manifestation of Gentile acceptance.

Two places, chapter 10:45 and 11:17, refer to this outpouring as a "gift" and not as the baptism, and it is nowhere directly called the baptism. When Peter declared that he remembered the word of the Lord, "Ye shall be baptized with the Holy Spirit," it was the promise made to the apostles which, according to Acts 1:5, was to be fulfilled—"not many days hence"—on the day of Pentecost. The statement of Peter in Acts 11:15, "as upon us at the beginning" is indicative of *manner* and not the *measure* of the reception—the passage says as a comparison, "the like gift"—like it in the manner by which the incident occurred, descending directly from heaven, which reminded Peter—he "remembered" the Pentecost occasion. Cornelius did not receive what the apostles had received; he did not know what the apostles knew; he could not do what the apostles did; and he was therefore not *endued* nor *clothed* with the power which the Holy Spirit baptism bestowed. He had no inspiration that the Holy Spirit baptism imparted; the gift that he received was an outward manifestation only, and did not continue with him, but was designed only to demonstrate to the Jews that the Gentiles were acceptable to God as gospel subjects. There was no reason why the Holy Spirit baptism should be employed for that end and purpose.

There can be no degrees in Holy Spirit baptism. Any two men baptized in the Holy Spirit would have equal measure of it. The apostles, including Paul, all had the same inspiration; one apostle did not have more of the baptism than another, and one was not less inspired than them all. On the point of receiving the apostolic powers and credentials, Paul declared in 2 Corinthians 11:5 that he was "not a whit behind the very chiefest apostle." There was no such thing as measures of Holy Spirit baptism, or of a limited Spirit baptism. If Cornelius had been baptized in the Holy Spirit he would have possessed all powers imparted by it and belonging to it, and he would not have been inferior to the apostles of Christ in any respect; he would have known all that the apostles knew, and could have done all that the apostles did, and it would not have been necessary for Peter to have told him anything.

THE PROPOSITION AND THE DEMONSTRATION

In answering the claims of men now who claim the Holy Spirit baptism, gospel preachers challenge them to do what the Spirit-baptized apostles did, and demonstrate their claims. As goes the proposition, so must be the demonstration. In my own experience in debate with a leading proponent of the Holy Spirit baptism, he had difficulty finding and reading his scripture passages, and became confused in his use of the notes prepared for his speeches. It was my pleasure to chide him about it: if he had what he claimed, he could have discarded his notes, and he could have surely quoted his scripture passages. The men that had the Holy Spirit baptism *wrote the Bible,* and if men had the Spirit baptism today they could write it again. Now, apply these powers of Holy Spirit baptism to the case of Cornelius and see the argument for it vaporize.

It has been somewhat of a wonder to me that some denominational preachers have not replied to the challenge for a demonstration of their claim by using this inconsistency on some of our preachers and thereby put them "over the barrel" on the case of Cornelius, for of certainty he did not possess the powers of the Holy Spirit baptism, nor could he have demonstrated what our own preachers have challenged the denominationalists to do in proof of the claim.

The fact in itself that Cornelius was enabled to speak with tongues was not a demonstration because the mere exercise of tongues was not a sign of Spirit baptism, but of a gift, such as prevailed among members of the churches during the time of spiritual endowments. There are numerous examples of the use of tongues for special purposes which had no connection at all with Holy Spirit baptism. The Old Testament records that Balaam's ass employed the tongue of a man, but I dare say that no one would claim that the ass was baptized in the Holy Spirit!

In a final word on the point, proof of the Holy Spirit baptism does not consist in the special endowments such as the spiritual gifts, or in the outward manifestation for special purposes as in the case of Cornelius, but it lies in the possession of the *Comforter* which the Lord Jesus Christ promised to his apostles, the plenary and verbal inspiration imparted to the apostles and to them alone. Any claim of Holy Spirit baptism by others than the apostles must be subject to demonstration, for *as goes the proposition, so must be the demonstration.*

THE LIKE GIFT

The statement of the text is that God gave the household of Cornelius *the like gift* that descended upon the apostles "at the beginning." Peter could as well have said *the same gift*—but it was not the same. By comparison, *the like faith* of the miraculous order was not the same in degree, for Paul said in Romans 12:23 that there were different measures of its possession and exercise. But the Holy Spirit baptism was not promised in degree, and was not possessed in different measures. It was that *clothing with power*—the Comforter, the Spirit of truth and inspiration, which was promised to the apostles—"Ye shall be clothed (endued) with power from on high"—and Cornelius was *not clothed with power.* If he had been *so clothed,* endued or imbued, he would have had inspiration himself, equal to the apostles, and not inferior to any of them, and therefore would have had no need of instruction from Peter with "words whereby he should be saved" or any other thing.

Furthermore, if the miracle at the house of Cornelius was the Holy Spirit baptism, since it is stated that the Spirit "fell on them"—the whole house of Cornelius, and upon all that were in his house on the occasion of Peter's address—it follows that they were all recipients of what the apostles received on Pentecost. Yet this miracle occurred before any of them had heard and believed the gospel, for in verse 15, Peter himself declares that the Spirit fell on them *as he began to speak;* but in Acts 15:7 Peter said they believed after having heard the word by his mouth. So if what happened at the house of Cornelius was Holy Spirit baptism, then this house full of unbelievers were all baptized in the Holy Spirit. That is what all of the "Holy Ghost baptism" cults claim, and have contended for in debate on the Holy Spirit, but we have not allowed them to get by with their false doctrine; it is out of harmony with the New Testament teaching on the workings of the Holy Spirit and the one purpose of Holy Spirit baptism. This case of the outpouring of the Spirit was clearly an outward miraculous manifestation to demonstrate, in a method similar to Pentecost, that the Gentiles were acceptable to God as gospel subjects and should be so received by all the Jews in the church everywhere, for it was nowhere else repeated.

If, then, it should be asked in what way the outpouring of the Spirit at the house of Cornelius differed from other special gifts of the Spirit, referred to in the New Testament as "spiritual gifts," it was in the fact that it was not imparted by the laying on of hands by the apostles; that it was not a source of knowledge to impart instruction, teaching, or edification and it did not continue with Cornelius and the hearers who were there. The respect in which it was unlike the gifts of the Spirit received by the spiritually endowed teachers is the precise respect in which it was *like* what occurred on Pentecost—in the *manner* of its reception only, in that it was not imparted but came direct from heaven as on Pentecost.

THE EXTENDED BENEFITS

The established fact that the baptism in the Holy Spirit was an endowment of inspiration, restricted to the apostles and confined to the apostolic age, does not imply that its benefits were thus limited; its effects include all who accept the teaching of the apostles, in that the blessings of the gospel which result from it are universal.

It has been difficult for people in general to make the proper discriminations between the special influences of the Holy Spirit by the special endowments of New Testament times, and the general working of the Holy Spirit through the word of God in the mind and heart. The effect of the Holy Spirit upon the apostles was its *baptism.* The direction of the Holy Spirit in the apostolic churches during the completion of the revealed word was called spiritual *gifts.* These provisional impartations were the tugboats of Christianity, serving the purpose to guide the ship of the church out of the channel into the open sea, where it sails on its own strength with the revealed word. These miraculous gifts were the scaffolding necessary to the building of the structure, but when the structure was completed the scaffolding was no longer needful and was removed. This was the argument of Paul in the thirteenth chapter of First Corinthians, in which the apostle explained that "when that which is perfect" should come, that which was "in part" should be done away. The "perfect" was God's completely revealed word; that which was "in part" was revelation in its incomplete stage. The revelation of the word of God was not brought into its completion at once. No one apostle delivered the whole of divine revelation; it was delivered in part, fragmentary, not all at one time. When the parts were gathered and brought together into one perfect whole, into the perfect revelation of the divine plan, then "that which is perfect" had come, no longer "in part" but in the whole, and the provisional order then ceased.

The thirteenth chapter of First Corinthians is an inspired treatise on the end of the special gifts and immediate operations of the Spirit within the church and its members. The conclusion of the chapter in the last verse reads: "And now abideth faith, hope, love, these three; but the greatest of these is love." This passage does not refer to heaven, and does not mean that "faith will be lost in sight, and hope will end in glad fruition." It refers to what would remain in the church when the order of special and provisional gifts had passed out. The exercise of special tongues, and direct knowledge, and inspired prophesying were all ready to end; but faith (the gospel system), and hope (in the promises of God), and love (the common bond)—all these would remain as the permanent order when the temporary and provisional endowments had all come to an end and vanished away.

Chapter Seven:
The Sin Against The Holy Spirit

There are two citations in the gospel records that deal with blaspheming the Holy Spirit: Matthew 12 and Mark 3. The Matthew text covers connecting verses from the twenty-fourth to the thirty-second, and the shorter passage in Mark includes verses twenty-two to twenty-nine. The power to deliver a victim from demon possession was considered by the Jews as the ultimate proof of divinity, but the scribes and the Pharisees had ascribed this power of Christ to the head of the demon world, Beelzebub. Jesus answered this charge by convicting them of inconsistency in having "Satan cast out Satan" or, as stated by Mark, having "Satan rise up against himself, and be divided" and thus bring an end to himself. Then Mark sounded this note of warning to the Jews: "He that shall blaspheme against the Holy Spirit hath never forgiveness, but is in danger of eternal damnation." Matthew puts it in the statement: "But the blasphemy against the Holy Spirit shall not be forgiven unto men." These words sound a note of the future from the then present, pointing to a time when the Holy Spirit would be offered to men to accept or reject. It is my considered opinion and conviction that these words of Christ take their place among the Pentecost pointers so predominant in his teaching from Jordan to Calvary. Before further elucidation of this concept, it is in order to examine some passages that have been misused to teach an unpardonable sin. Many people entertain apprehensions that they may have committed such a sin and despair of obedience to the gospel for salvation, but such fears are the best proof that they are still open to repentance and pardon.

IMPOSSIBLE TO RENEW

A frequently misconstrued passage is Hebrews 6:4-6: 'For it is impossible for those who were once enlightened....if they shall fall away, to renew them again unto repentance." The entire context of the Hebrew epistle is the argument of Paul against a mass apostasy from the new covenant to the Mosaic law, a reversion from Christianity to Judaism. The first verses of chapter six enumerate a category of ordinances that once had their place in the elder dispensation which had been nullified at the cross and had no part in the new covenant. The mention of the first principles in verse 1, referred to the rudiments or elements of Judaism as in Galatians 4:1-4, which were fundamental or rudimentary to the new covenant, in the same way that Paul in Galatians 3:24-25 affirmed that "the law was our schoolmaster (tutor) to bring us unto Christ." The Hebrews were exhorted to leave these first principles of the Mosaic law, or Judaism, and "go on unto perfection"—in the new covenant. Identifying the obsolete ordinances the apostle named *repentance from dead works*—the sacrificial system; *faith toward* God—before Christ came; the *doctrine of baptisms*—the plural washings of the Mosaic law; laying on of hands—the priestly ceremonies of the tabernacle services; and of *resurrection of the dead*—reviving the dead ordinances of Judaism; and of *eternal judgment*—the annual renewing of sins without remission. The existing threat was the defection from the new covenant to the abrogated Law of Moses, which appeared to have endangered even some of the spiritually endowed teachers among them. But if they should thus fall away from the new covenant and return to the old order, it would be impossible for them to obtain the renewing again unto repentance from the relegated altars. The Mosaic altars were no longer efficacious, and there was nothing to which they could return. The impossibility of being renewed unto repentance of this passage refers to the obsolete altars of Judaism and not to an unpardonable sin that someone may mysteriously commit.

THERE REMAINETH NO MORE SACRIFICE

The same application must be made of the warning in Hebrews 10:26: "For if we sin willfully after that we have received a knowledge of the truth, there remaineth no more sacrifice for sins." Under the threat of persecution described in verses 32 to 39, some of the Hebrew Christians had *forsaken the assembly,* which meant the abandonment of the new covenant. The Lord's Supper is the new covenant in his blood, Jesus declared in Matthew 26:28. To forsake a thing means to renounce it and abandon it. The urgent need of a "more and more" exhortation was based upon "the day approaching," which undoubtedly refers to the day of their persecutions, as "the present distress" of the Corinthian passage. To say that Paul meant for them to exhort each other more on Saturday than the Monday before is too trite for this context. The reference to the *assembly* means the first day of the week, and the day approaching referred to an imminent, ominous day—the impending persecutions, as verses 32 to 39 clearly show. The knowledge of the truth in verse 26 means the new covenant, and the sinning willfully referred to abandoning the knowledge of the new covenant and returning to Judaism; and the consequence was: "There remaineth no more sacrifice for sin"—that is, the whole sacrificial system was obsolete and the altars of Judaism no longer provided atonement for sin. Reverting to the same persuasion in chapter 13:10, the apostle said: "We have an altar, whereof they have no right to eat which serve the tabernacle." Our altar is Jesus Christ, and those who returned to the Mosaic system, represented by the tabernacle, were cut off from the new covenant altar. Verses 26 to 29 of chapter 10 give a final verdict on the fearful consequences of renouncing the new covenant. But what is commonly called the unpardonable sin is not implied in these verses.

A SIN UNTO DEATH

A final passage, misunderstood and misapplied, is 1 John 5:16: "If any man see his brother sin a sin which is not unto death, he shall ask, and he shall give him life for them that sin not unto death. There is a sin unto death: I do not say that he shall pray for it." It is evident that the use of the pronoun "he" all through this passage refers to the man who prays for the sinning brother. The statement "he shall give him life" indicates the exercise of spiritual gifts and connects this passage with the "effectual fervent prayer of a righteous man" of James 5:14-16 in the exercise of the spiritual gifts listed in 1 Corinthians 12. The passage presents two classes of men and a classification of sins. It is not a single sin not unto death, and is therefore not a single sin that is unto death. The man who sins not unto death is a brother who is not an habitual sinner, and he maintains a life of general rectitude and of repentance when he sins. The man who sins unto death, sins with no restraint and without feelings that lead to repentance. The first man comes under the rule of Galatians 6:1 where the "spiritual"—that is, the ones who possessed the spiritual gifts—were to use their offices to "restore such an one." So here, the spiritual man prays for the brother sinning in some way against "the brotherhood" mentioned by John, but with the disposition to repent, and as stated in James 5:15, "the Lord shall raise him up" and his sins "shall be forgiven him." The prayer of *faith* is evidently a reference to the spiritual gift mentioned in the twelfth and thirteenth chapters of First Corinthians in reference to the exercise of spiritual gifts. But praying for the one who has no sense of guilt or penitence was not within the endowments of the spiritually gifted men to perform, and his sins would inevitably end in his spiritual death. Jesus Christ expressed the same principle in addressing the Jews: "I go my way, and ye shall seek me and shall die in your sins: whither I go ye cannot come."

The sinning man, who does not turn away from the habits of

sin, cannot effectually pray, or be prayed for, but "abideth in death," and he lives in the possibility of incurring its final doom. But there is not in any of these passages the connotations of an unpardonable sin.

THE HOLY SPIRIT'S AGE

The Lord said in Matthew's statement on blaspheming the Holy Spirit that it should not be forgiven "neither in this world, neither in the world to come." The whole context indicates that the phrase "this world" had reference to the Holy Spirit's age which the language was anticipating. It could have no application to the Jewish age or the period of the Lord's ministry for neither was the dispensation of the Holy Spirit. In Ephesians 1:21 the same expression occurs, and there *this world* referred to the gospel age, and *the world to come* referred to eternity. That is the significance of these phrases in Matthew 12:32. The language anticipated the dispensation of the Holy Spirit beginning on the day of Pentecost. The subject was the Holy Spirit and the reference to *this world* in that connection meant the Holy Spirit's age or dispensation, and to blaspheme the work of the Holy Spirit, when his testimony was offered to men in the completion of God's redemptive plan, would constitute a final rejection of all divine overtures, and would have no clemency in this last dispensation of time, and no mitigation in eternity.

With emphasis on the finality of this blasphemy, Jesus said: "Whosoever speaketh a word against the Son of man, it shall be forgiven him, but whosoever speaketh against the Holy Spirit, it shall not be forgiven him." There could be no reason why speaking against the Christ should be less fatal than speaking against the Holy Spirit, or that speaking against the Holy Spirit, should be more mortal than speaking against Jesus Christ, except for one thing: the element of time, of dispensation, of the gospel age, and of the Holy Spirit's testimony. The rejection of Christ during his earthly and personal ministry was not final. But the repudiation of the Holy Spirit in the dispensation of his testimony to "reprove the world of sin, of righteousness, and of judgment" (John 16:8), would be the final act of rejection. Jesus was speaking of the present with reference to himself, and of the future as it applied to the Holy Spirit. There could be no difference now in the rejection of the Holy Spirit and the rejection of Jesus Christ, and there are numerous passages to sustain this assertion.

The record of Mark says, "he that shall blaspheme against the Holy Spirit hath never forgiveness, but is in danger of eternal damnation." It is the language of the future—*danger of eternal damnation.* The parallel with Mark's record of the Great Commission is compelling: *"He that believeth not shall be damned"—and* he that blasphemes the Holy Spirit by a repudiation of his testimony *shall be in danger of damnation.* It reverts to the connection in Matthew's record between the establishment of the kingdom and the blaspheming of the Holy Spirit—the sin of repudiating the Spirit's testimony in the gospel age. There are numerous passages that use this word *blaspheme* in that very sense. The apostle mentioned blaspheming the word of God in Titus 2:5; and blaspheming the doctrine in 1 Tim. 6:1; which was noted in item *twenty-nine* under the section heading, *The Spirit and The Word.* There could be no valid distinction between blaspheming the Spirit and blaspheming the word of the Spirit.

THE PENTECOST PIVOT

The pivot on which all of the teaching turns is Pentecost. In the scope of these premises there is but one logical conclusion: the blasphemy of the Holy Spirit must of necessity have started from Pentecost. The connection with the kingdom in the Lord's own statements, the coming of the kingdom with the power and the Spirit on the day of Pentecost-these were all Pentecost pointers; and upon that occasion, in fulfillment of all the prophets had foretold and that the teaching of Christ had anticipated, the Holy Spirit's testimony was offered to all mankind to accept or reject.

In the acceptance of it the Word of God was glorified, and in the repudiation of it the Holy Spirit was blasphemed.

But the deliberate repudiation of the Holy Spirit's testimony is not the only way that men sin against the Spirit. There is an apathy toward the Holy Spirit's appeals which if continued will result in the same *eternal damnation.* The law of atrophy decrees that a member of the body unused, nature removes. An eye may be punched out, and that would be an unpardonable sin against the sight; but the eyes may be closed with a bandage impervious to light and in time the optic nerve will have become an insensate thread, never to see again—the slower method, but the same result. The arm may be amputated, but it may also be bound to the side without use for a certain length of time and the withering process would destroy it beyond restoration—again, the slower method, but the same result. It is so spiritually. The apostle mentioned some who were "past feeling," and others who had "their conscience seared with a hot iron." This was not so with them always, it was the progressive state resulting from continued rejection of the word of God. The same apostle exhorted certain men to "grieve not the Holy Spirit of God"—and that is done by withstanding the inspired testimony of the spirit. Stephen accused the Jews of resisting the Holy Spirit—by disobedience to the Holy Spirit's teaching. Paul exhorted the Thessalonians to "quench not the Spirit"—by extinguishing from within the word of God which he had by the inspiration of the Spirit preached to them. The Holy Spirit's earnest appeal to prompt action says: "Today if ye will hear his voice, harden not your hearts."

To the Corinthians the apostle said that the gospel of Christ to one is "the savour of death unto death"; and to another "a savour of life unto life"—to all who reject the gospel it is the deadly smell that ends in the death of the soul; to all who accept its promises it is the spiritual fragrance that perfumes the soul and leads to endless life. The same process that hardens wax will soften clay, and the same gospel that saves the believer will damn the unbeliever. "He that believeth and is baptized shall be saved; but he that believeth not shall be damned." These passages are the perpetual persuasions to all men not to sin against the Holy Spirit.

Conclusion

The principles postulated in this discussion of *The Mission and Medium of the Holy Spirit* embody basic doctrine and cannot be waived aside or cast away with the indifferent attitude that brethren have always had disagreements and held divergent views on various nonessential issues. The Holy Spirit question is doctrinal; it involves the gospel system in its entirety. To the same extent that the doctrine of the direct operation of the Holy Spirit in conversion is related to the dogmas of original sin and hereditary total depravity, the theory of the immediate indwelling and direct possession of the personal Holy Spirit is related to the dogma of the impossibility of apostasy—for the personal inhabitation of the Holy Spirit would mean personal Holy Spirit guidance in thoughts, words, and deeds, the logical consequence of which would necessarily prohibit and prevent apostasy, making it impossible for one so possessed to fall from grace. If not, why not—if it is not true, the indwelling personal Holy Spirit would be of no aid or help in the time of temptation but would abandon one at the time of his fall to re-enter him after his recovery—in him and out of him, entering and re-entering him! Both the direct operation and personal possession of the Holy Spirit theories are the outgrowths of the false doctrines of "original sin" and "the sinful nature of man," whether it is admitted or not, and its consequence is the impossibility of apostasy—once in grace, *always in grace*—else the personal Holy Spirit possession is ineffectual in that he fails the indwelling subject in the hour of need.

Of all the religious bodies in all the world to become involved in such theological error, the members of the churches of Christ should be the last to be thus confused. It indicates a tragic lapse of that indoctrination in our day which was known in the generation past. The only remedy is a return to the *first principles gospel preaching* that planted the church in our land and produced its growth. In another generation such preaching will become a lost art, and such preachers a vanished breed, if the preachers today do not go into immediate action and make the old gospel ring over hill and plain, in town and country, crossroads and cities, whether in joint-efforts called a *campaign* or on the local level of a *gospel meeting,* or radio broadcasting on the national hook-up or on the local scale—if the full distinctive gospel is not preached through these mediums they are no more than big promotions destructive of the scriptural character and distinctive identity of the New Testament church.

When a so-called *campaign* is more or less than a wide scale gospel meeting it is not a *campaign for Christ* but a compromise of *the cause of Christ.* It is a matter of general knowledge now that the line between the New Testament church and denominationalism, between truth and error, is not being drawn; and that the sermons being preached in these campaigns, with little exception, could be delivered in the Billy Graham crusades. The results reported in hundreds of "responses" are of the same meaningless type—they are not gospel additions at all. The full gospel is not being preached in these promotional campaigns and the New Testament church is not being set forth to the gathered thousands—and the time is running out.

The time is now. May the preachers of the gospel realize it and go forth in unison to do battle for the truth, and may the elders of the churches support them—for they will need it. In the words of God to Gideon: "Go in this thy might and thou shalt save Israel."

Commendatory

From L.N. Moody, Walnut Ridge, Arkansas:

The teaching contained in this book could not have appeared in print at a more appropriate time. Many of our preachers, elders, and teachers have not given sufficient study to all parts of the subject discussed in it. Brother Wallace never leaves a subject until every erroneous idea has been exposed by the light of God's word. While it was necessary to deal with some arguments in the Greek, to show the error taught by some who had resorted to that language, he at no time failed to prove his point by the Bible. If the Spirit works in a direct dynamic power beyond and in addition to the Word, then the Bible is not sufficient and does not "thoroughly furnish us," as each person would be guided separately within himself. This is exactly the teaching of the denominations whose preachers were met and this doctrine exposed by gospel preachers in the past. The young preachers now, and all who plan to preach, should be grounded in Bible teaching on the Holy Spirit subject, and every gospel subject; but it seems that the administrations of our schools are not keeping watch over what is being taught to our young people. This book should be in the home of all members of the Lord's church. One will not be misled on this subject who has this book in his hand.

From George W. DeHoff, DeHoff Publications, Murfreesboro, Tennessee:

Since 1930 I have been hearing Foy E. Wallace Jr. preach. I followed, with interest, his presentation and defense of the Truth on premillennialism, instrumental music, and hobbyism. Now in the years of his maturity, as the scion of a worthy heritage, he is presenting the truth about the operation of the Holy Spirit in conviction and sanctification. Brother Wallace, in this book, teaches the truth and will arm Bible students—especially young preachers—to meet this latest error threatening the truth of the gospel. All believe the Holy Spirit dwells in Christians. The question is how? The answer is through the hearing of faith, the Word of God.

From Carroll B. Ellis, Chairman Department of Speech, David Lipscomb University, Nashville, Tennessee:

When my wife and I were on our honeymoon, we stopped in Colorado Springs to worship. Because in the past we had seen a sign "Church of Christ" on a building and had entered to find it was not, we were a little skeptical as we went into the meeting house. As we sat down, I picked up a song book, and we looked at it together. I whispered, "This is a loyal congregation because they are using a song book published by Foy E. Wallace Jr." I would not want to put too much faith in any man; but through the years, I have had a growing appreciation of brother Foy E. Wallace Jr. Few men have dedicated themselves so completely and as effectively to the advancement of New Testament Christianity. He is not a sensationalist, but there has always been something exciting about his preaching. The simplicity, thoroughness, and dynamic quality in his preaching and writing are always evident. While he has the ability to hold an audience as few men do, it is not by tricks or fake emotion, but by proclaiming clearly and boldly God's word. This past year (1967), he has spoken at the Brookmeade Church of Christ in Nashville, Tennessee, where it is my privilege to preach; and has spoken at David Lipscomb University. On these occasions, as in the past, his greatness was evident. He has never been a more powerful preacher than he is now.

I am happy to commend to you this publication on the Holy Spirit. The force of it lies not in novelty or in newness. Foy E. Wallace Jr. is standing with Dr. T.W. Brents, David Lipscomb, Tolbert Fanning, and Alexander Campbell in a basic position which was fundamental to the success of the Restoration Movement. The church has grown under this type of preaching. The real power is not in Foy E. Wallace, nor in any man, but in the faithfulness of the message to the Word of God.

From Leroy Brownlow, Brownlow Publishing Company, Fort Worth, Texas:

I appreciate your articles on the Holy Spirit and found them very invigorating. They deserve the widest readership. The topic is basic and fundamental with deep-seated roots and far-reaching fruits. Our understanding or misunderstanding here can take us a long way on the road to truth or error, thus the study is ever timely, but especially for this present time. In these enlightening lessons your ripe scholarship, analytical mind, deep perception, love of the truth and sincere straight-forwardness shine like a diamond in a world that is rapidly becoming benighted by a lack of such qualities. I commend them.

Some have been hiding behind the paper wall of

academic freedom. Trustees in our schools have the same responsibility to maintain sound teaching in classes, programs, and lectureships that elders have to maintain sound doctrine in classes, programs, and lectureships—that is, if we are going to run Christian schools; for a Christian is a defender of the faith. Sound doctrine is not just a cloak to be worn on church premises and then exchange it on college campus for some of these new, elastic stretchable garments which permit unrestricted freedom.

The Holy Spirit articles are excellent—good logic. They cannot be classified as Lenten messages at this season, because they are so full of meat. The idea now being taught by some brethren that the Word is not sufficient is in effect the old doctrine that the Word of God is a dead letter, and these brethren do not have anything to support them in their claim for the direct operations of the Holy Spirit. All their proofs are only assumptions. "The legs of the lame are unequal."

From Roy J. Hearn, Director Getwell School of Preaching, Memphis, Tennessee:

For over half a century the author of this work has been a stalwart soldier of the cross and an able defender of the faith. His heart has ever been loyal to the word of God. His name is a synonym for sound doctrine. Nearly a lifetime of diligent study and wide experience make brother Wallace eminently qualified to deal with present issues concerning the Holy Spirit. No man living is mare distinguished as a thinker and writer than Foy E. Wallace Jr.

In the contents of this book the author, with mater

hand and trenchant pen, has traced out and explained the nature and work of the Holy Spirit, making it admirably adapted to the understanding of all who love the truth. The chapters are decidedly well written, and lucidly explain the subject in hand. This work deals with the Holy Spirit in a safe and most reliable manner, making the truth shine forth.

In clearing away the perplexities and confusion, and exposing the errors espoused by some brethren relative to the nature and work of the Holy Spirit, the present work is the most valuable treatment of the subject in print. Not only by his keen logical reasoning, but by appealing to the supreme authority of the Scriptures he has utterly demolished the false positions held by some prominent brethren today, as well as the sectarian world. On the subjects in hand, passage by passage, it is the finest and most complete work available. Those who love the truth, and stand for the purity of the gospel, should strive to see that it is distributed to every member of the church.

From Hulen L. Jackson, Trinity Heights Church, Dallas, Texas:

The Mission and Medium of the Holy Spirit—what a subject and where could you find one better qualified to discuss it than Foy E. Wallace Jr.? These articles I have read carefully and commend most highly. The sects are greatly disturbed and to some extent divided over questions concerning the Holy Spirit today. Some leading lights among them are advocating the personal indwelling and the miraculous possessions of gifts in today's church. Brethren are disturbed over these matters and the subjects needs discussion from the pulpit, from the press, and in the Bible classroom. We have very little material in print on this vital theme up to now and for this reason also I rejoice that these articles by brother Wallace are being made available. The cost is such that churches can and should purchase them in large bundles, distribute them to all their families, and have all of their adult classes study the booklet. If we do not, the church will suffer greatly from the error being taught by others today. The truth must be taught. Here is a convenient way of doing so.

From Wallace Gooch, Hudson & Elm Church, Altus, Oklahoma:

This shaft of light from the poignant pen of Foy Wallace brilliantly illuminates a beclouded issue at a critical time in the life of the church. The clear thinking, the rich scholarship, and the forceful logic of brother Wallace was never more strikingly demonstrated than in this monumental work. I recommend it without reservation. The study of it is a must for every preacher, elder, and teacher in the brotherhood. It should be used as a textbook for class study in every congregation. Amidst the shifting sands of current teaching, this book is *solid ground.*

From W.F. Cawyer, Elder Highland Church, Abilene, Texas:

It has been my pleasure to know Foy E. Wallace Jr., as well as his deceased brother, Cled E. Wallace, whose writings I had the good fortune to read for many years. I regarded him as one of the safest writers of the brotherhood. The Wallace family has been a family of faithful preachers, opposing any and all opposition to the truth with power and conviction. My personal convictions are that Foy's articles on the Holy Spirit are in general sound and thought provoking.

From H.A. Dobbs, Memorial Church, Houston, Texas:

Thank God for Foy Wallace. Your articles on the Holy Spirit are tremendous! 1 am looking forward to future articles on this and other subjects. We have a big fight on our hands and you are just the man to lead us.

From Delmar Owens, Eastside Church of Christ, Tulsa, Oklahoma:

It is an honor for me to be privileged to lend my endorsement to the outstanding work of brother Foy E. Wallace Jr. on the subject of the Holy Spirit. He has presented the truth on this subject in such a scholarly way as to show his absolute faith in the inerrant and all-sufficient word of God. The subject matter covered in this book deserves a wide acceptance among the faithful brethren of the Lord in these days, when, in my judgment, the church must militantly fight for her scriptural identity.

From Hershel Dyer, Tenth & Rockford Church, Tulsa, Oklahoma:

We are once again, as we have been many times in the past, placed under obligation to our highly esteemed brother, Foy E. Wallace Jr. His timely and scholarly writing on *The Mission and Medium of the Holy Spirit* will long live to bless and edify lovers of truth. His many years of deep study and his wide range of experience in refuting the diversity of errors concerning the Holy Spirit prepared us to expect the very ablest discussion of the subject from him. He has well gratified our expectations. Mightily he exalts the Spirit as the author of the word of truth and that selfsame word as the all-sufficient means whereby the Spirit convicts, converts and sanctifies men! He takes his refuge in the impregnable rock of Holy Scripture and men should think long and soberly before they attack that fortress.

From Lester W. Fisher, Myrtle Creek, Oregon:

God bless you! Thank God for your effective pen. The articles on the Holy Spirit in the *Firm Foundation* are fine and true to His word. And they will do untold good. Some of our professors are taking a sectarian stand on this question and is beginning to show up in the preaching of those whom they train. I never fail to preach on the Holy Spirit in every meeting, sometimes two or three times. I have most of the writings of R.L. Whiteside.

From Glenn A. Posey, Hillview Church, Birmingham, Alabama:

Your articles on the Holy Spirit have been edifying to me. I am now looking at your Article No. 5 on The Mission and Medium of the Holy Spirit, which contains the truth, if I am a true judge of the Scriptures.

For me, a young gospel preacher, to tell a warrior of the faith, like you, that the articles are the truth might not mean too much, however, it is my desire that you would either put these in tract form or some other distributionary media so that literally thousands of young gospel preachers could have access to these great truths.

Brother Wallace, may God bless you for your stand of the truth and may your life be richer and fuller as the years go by.

From James L. Russell, Garden Grove, California:

Your series of articles on the Holy Spirit currently appearing in the *Firm Foundation* have helped me tremendously. Words cannot adequately express the gratitude in my heart to you and our heavenly Father for those enlightening commentaries.

From Charles E. Maxwell, Cookeville, Tennessee:

I want to express to you my personal feelings for the wonderful, scriptural lessons on the Holy Spirit and its work. I have never read any better material on any subject that I enjoyed more.

From William Kay Moser, Muscatine, Iowa:

I want to thank you for your articles in the *Firm Foundation* lately. I have never needed anything worse (that I know of), and I have certainly appreciated them. The other that appeared on the same subject never got away from leaving something-better-felt-than-told, and nothing I could base on the Bible. You have. Your straight-forwardness, no-respect-of-persons type of teaching I appreciate, and all should.

From R.G. Hatter, Deleon, Texas:

Ask the professors that in case one might be lost, if he would still have the indwelling Holy Spirit, if he could lose it, or if God recalls it. These men belong in the Baptist camp. I am an old man, born in the century before this one, and have been a member of the church since 1917, and that is not long enough for me to swap the truth for Baptist doctrine on the Holy Spirit or anything else.

From W.R. Craig, Elk City, Oklahoma

I believe that your greatest work is now being done for the cause. I thank God often that you are still with us and your voice is being heard. Your articles on the Holy Spirit have been the salvation of many a young preacher in this area. They were being led astray until your voice was raised in behalf of truth. I do not think anybody, Ph.D., or whatnot, can answer or refute them.

From Homer H. Bryant, elder, Seminole, Oklahoma:

I have enjoyed your articles on the Holy Spirit in the Firm Foundation. It is hard for me to understand where some brethren get the ideas they have on so many important subjects. I am afraid some are reading too many books written by so-called scholars of the denominational world. I often feel so thankful that I had the privilege of being associated with such wonderful brethren as your father, brother Cled, and brother C.R. Nichol. They did so much for me. The church of our Lord misses such men in this age. You have done so much to help keep down false doctrine and are continuing to do so. May the Lord bless you and give you many more years to live.

From W.P. Jolly, Lakeshore Church, Shreveport, Louisiana:

Great issues require great men to resolve them. The church has not produced a more capable thinker than brother Wallace, nor one more skilled in the articulate expression of his thoughts. He has that rare ability to cut through mountains of extraneous and irrelevant matter and strike with swift and unerring precision the exact focal point of controversy. And the Mission and Medium of the Holy Spirit question is that point, and to it our attention has been directed. These articles are worthy of serious and prayerful study and represent no small effort on the part of brother Wallace whom we hold in highest esteem both as preacher and friend. It is our fervent hope that this book will enjoy a wide circulation among the brethren. We are entering the greatest battle that the church has faced since the beginning of the Restoration. The undertow of liberal thought is running strong.

From Hugo McCord, Vice-President Oklahoma Christian College, Oklahoma City, Oklahoma:

A third of a century ago I became convinced, and still am, that Foy E. Wallace Jr., was and is committed so to Jesus that he will allow no human being to come between him and Jesus. On a few doctrinal matters, very few, I have disagreed, tremblingly, with his conclusions, but always with the respect and love a son owes a father. One of those few divergences is on the proposition he has sought to sustain in his book *The Mission and Medium of the Holy Spirit.*

However, his book is bound to dispel and dissipate extreme and untenable positions in regard to the Holy Spirit. In a time when not only denominationalists but brethren are advocating tongue talking and direct leadings by the Holy Spirit, his work will do much to restore normalcy and common sense. I believe that the Holy Spirit dwells in my physical body (the one in which fornication could be committed (1 Corinthians 6:18-20) as a certification that I am God's child (Galatians 4:6), but I could not know he is there unless the Bible had told me. His indwelling is not sensuous: it cannot be felt. The Holy Spirit dwelt in the Ephesians (Ephesians 1:13), but their being strengthened with power through his Spirit in the inward man (Ephesians 3:16) was not by that indwelling, but by their reading and applying to themselves the book of Ephesians (specifically note the strength of his might through putting on the armor of God, Ephesians 6:10-18) and by reading and applying to themselves the letter to the church at Ephesus (Revelation 2:1-7). If all brethren would carefully read brother Wallace's new book, they would forever be rid of alleged mysterious feelings and guidings falsely imputed to the Holy Spirit.

Response to the undue and undeserved eulogiums is with deepest appreciation and reciprocal sentiments, and the things that have been said warm the cockles of an "older preacher's" heart. The 1 Corinthians 6:18-20 passage does not yield the idea of the personal Holy Spirit indwelling in the physical body—there are legions of moral men not members of the church who do not and would not commit fornication because of moral conscience, but all will surely admit that the Holy Spirit does not personally reside in the physical body of a non-Christian. Verse 20 states that the physical body is also God's, but it is not claimed that God dwells personally in the physical body. The passage merely states the fact, and the question of the how is answered by other passages. There is no basis for an assumption that the Holy Spirit dwells in the body in any sense differing from the how that God dwells in the body—and that is through the doing of his will according to the teaching of God by the Holy Spirit. The personal indwelling of the Holy Spirit in the physical body is not the certification of being a child of God—the word of God is my own certification of that fact, and there is no other.

It has been shown on pages 92-94 of this treatise that Galatians 4:6-7 refers to the spirit of sons, not to the Holy Spirit, as verse 7 clearly shows; and Ephesians 1:13 is discussed in detail on pages 76-80; and the phrase "strengthened with might" by the Holy Spirit in Ephesians 3:16 is equated with the same phrase in Colossians 1:11, by the knowledge of "the truth of the gospel" (verses 5-11). The admission that "the strength of his might" was received by the Ephesians through reading and applying the teaching of the Ephesian epistle—Ephesians 6:10-18 and Revelation 2:7—surrenders the argument for the personal indwelling of the Spirit, for the teaching and the word are the same thing. By the logical conclusions from these admissions of my devoted and equally estimable friend, he has himself dissipated the disagreement; and I have not merely "sought to sustain the proposition that the Holy Spirit works upon and within us only through the word"—I *have* sustained it.

From the full depths of my heart, gratitude overflows for the generous expressions and good words that have come to me which could not be conveyed to the readers of these pages. May we all together join the refrain of the Psalmist: "Guide me with thy counsel, and afterward receive me to glory."

—FOY E. WALLACE JR.

www.ingramcontent.com/pod-product-compliance
Lightning Source LLC
Chambersburg PA
CBHW070105080526
44586CB00013B/1191